D0913094

SUPER AGAIN!

The Official Book of the Super Bowl XL Champion Pittsburgh Steelers

Copyright ©2006 by the Pittsburgh Steelers and Curtis Publishing

To the reader ...

"When we stink, you have to tell the truth, so when we tell people we're good they'll believe us."

That's what Dan Rooney said to me in the summer of 1988 when *Steelers Digest* was born and I was hired to be its editor. There was a lot of truth that had to be told that season, when the Steelers were 2-10 at Thanksgiving on the way to a 5-11 finish, and he let it all happen. That was 18 years ago, and there has been a lot more good than bad to report between then and now, but that still never changed the mandate.

Dan Rooney believes Steelers fans are the best in the world. He knows they are loyal, knowledgeable about the game, and that they travel all over the country to watch their team play, and *Steelers Digest* was created as a way to communicate directly with them. To be certain, I have fumbled the facts occasionally, and false-started on some opinions, and even stepped over the fine line once or twice, but Dan Rooney never engaged in censorship, he never demanded right-of-refusal on anything before it was published.

"Super Again!" is the story of the 2005 Pittsburgh Steelers, and as you read this book you're going to be told a tale of a football team made up of special men who accomplished something great. You can believe it.

— **Bob Labriola**

About the Writer:

Bob Labriola has been editor of **Steelers Digest** *since its inception in July 1988. A Pittsburgh native, Labriola is also a contributor on the Steelers Radio Network and appears on shows produced by SteelersTV that are broadcast on the NFL Network. Labriola worked for the* **Greensburg Tribune-Review** *and the* **Indiana (Pa.) Gazette** *before coming to* **Steelers Digest***. He and his wife, Marianne, live in the North Hills.*

SUPER AGAIN!

The Official Book
of the Super Bowl XL Champion
Pittsburgh Steelers

Written by
BOB LABRIOLA

Photo Editor
MIKE FABUS

Creative Director
ARMANDO MATO

An Official Publication of the Pittsburgh Steelers
Daniel M. Rooney, *Chairman*
Arthur J. Rooney II, *President*
Tony Quatrini, *Director of Marketing*

© 2006
By Curtis Publishing

Thomas N. Curtis, *Publisher*
Andrew E. Cohen, *General Manager*
Alain Poupart, *Associate Editor*
Teresa Varley, *Assistant Editor*
Adam Glassman, *Copy Editor*

All rights reserved.
No part of this book may be reproduced
or transmitted in any form without written
permission from the Pittsburgh Steelers
and Curtis Publishing.

ISBN: 0-9702677-9-7
(Hard Bound)

0-9702677-8-9
(Soft Bound)

Printed in the
United States of America

Table of Contents

Foreword

First, let me say how proud I am of the 2005 Pittsburgh Steelers for what they accomplished, for winning the Super Bowl and doing it the hard way, with three road wins in the AFC playoffs. For that alone, this team deserves a special place in Steelers history and, for that matter, NFL history.

The credit belongs to so many people. An outstanding group of players. The best coaching staff in the NFL. And, of course, the fans who provide the greatest support of any fan group in the NFL. This isn't just my opinion. This view is shared by many people who not only see the devotion of Steelers fans at Heinz Field but wherever we play on the road. These fans are truly the Steelers Nation. It was gratifying, though not surprising, to see so many Steelers fans at Ford Field for the Super Bowl. It is something that should make us all proud.

We are hopeful that this book will bring you enjoyment for years to come. We have so much to celebrate and to be thankful for after this season. Our desire is for the pictures and stories in this book to serve as a reminder of some of the great moments that took place, the way this team refused to lose again after it got to a 7-5 record and the manner in which different players rose to the occasion in every game.

There are so many wonderful memories captured in these pages. From the important steps taken in the regular season to the huge victories in Cincinnati, Indianapolis and Denver in the playoffs, to the Super Bowl win over Seattle. It was a season that contained a storybook ending, and thus it's a season deserving a book of this kind.

But without the unyielding support from our fans, none of this would have been possible. I can't tell you enough times how grateful I am for your support and how much we want you to continue to be a part of our success in the future.

So enjoy the wonderful trip through the 2005 season that this book provides, and I can only hope it brings you a great sense of satisfaction for years to come.

Keep rooting for the Steelers.

Dan Rooney
HOF 2000

Dan Rooney

Bill Cowher

A strong, consistent leader

In the billion-dollar industry that professional football has become, coaches' careers are evaluated, those careers ultimately are defined, by what they win. The games, the division titles their teams accumulate are nice, the playoff berths they earn are appreciated. But in the National Football League, legacies are labeled by championships. Rings on the finger. Trophies in the lobby.

Only 22 men have coached a team to a Super Bowl championship, and Bill Cowher is one of them. His career now tells the story of the hometown kid who grew up in a neighborhood 10 minutes from where the Pittsburgh Steelers dominated the NFL from 1972-79 and then became the coach who returned that team to the perch of a champion. The last part, though, the winning the championship part, only can be told by going back to 2003.

The Steelers won Super Bowl XL for a lot of reasons, through the contributions of many. But there are certain reasons that were more important and certain people who made more of a difference, and Bill Cowher is the one who brought those elements and people all together, and he did it in the midst of a difficult time in his career.

The 2003 season was destined to be a bad one for the Steelers. In simple terms, they had lost their way. The offense had been enticed down the wrong path and the defense had strayed too far from its roots. The team lost five straight to arrive at the midway point at 2-6, and

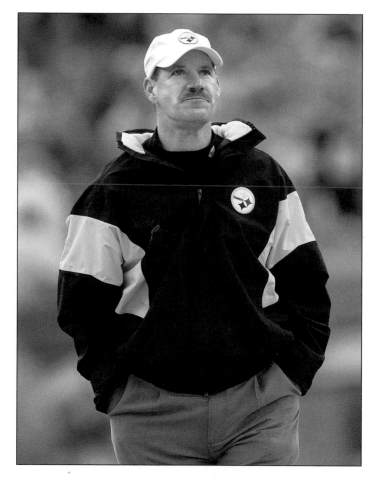

then it played win-one, lose-one from there to finish with a record that tied the previous low-water mark of Cowher's career, a record that gets NFL coaches fired. It was during those miserable weeks that Bill Cowher cemented a relationship of trust and respect with the same core of players who filled the roster the Steelers would bring to Detroit for the climax of the 2005 NFL season.

Cowher played those games to win at the end of 2003, each one of those nothing games in November and December that could have been used as the start of the next pre-season. He played them to win, and because he didn't quit his players didn't, either; from then on, whenever they had to accept a decision he made, they knew his only agenda was to win football games. That, they could accept. For that, they would be willing to give everything they had.

When that 6-10 season ended, Cowher found himself in the situation of having to replace both coordinators, and he took advantage of it. He first made sure Ken Whisenhunt shared his belief in the benefits of an offense that could and would run the football even when opponents knew it was coming. And he brought back Dick LeBeau to fix the defense, a move that said a lot about Bill Cowher, both as a football coach and a man.

A defensive backs coach on Cowher's inaugural staff with the Steelers, LeBeau had the right situation and the right personnel to perfect his zone-blitz ideas, and when coordinator Dom Capers left to be a head coach after the 1994 season, LeBeau was promoted. After the 1996 season, LeBeau left the Steelers for what turned out to be the same job with a much inferior Cincinnati Bengals team, and some head coaches in the NFL would look upon that as a slap in the face. But Cowher never engaged in any of that, he always praised LeBeau when asked and genuinely respected the games against the Bengals when they competed as rival head coaches.

The reasons Dick LeBeau and the Steelers parted ways at the end of the 1996 season might not even be known fully to the men directly involved, but Bill Cowher never allowed it to become petty. So, when he was looking for a coordinator who would return the defense to its attacking roots and LeBeau happened to be available because he was finished with a consulting post in Buffalo after being fired in Cincinnati, Cowher knew who was the best man for the job and made the offer. Just like the team's core of players, LeBeau knew what Cowher's agenda was, and he accepted happily.

With the offensive and defensive ideologies back in place, the next chore was selling the players. That was the time in early 2004 when Bill Cowher started talking about what he called "re-establishing the mind-set," which turned out to be code for a physical training camp where every practice was used to hone the players' natural competitiveness into a hard, sharp edge.

Then came the 2004 season, and the winning began. The fourth 15-1 regular season in NFL history was a testament to the way Cowher re-established the Steelers' mind-set. Every week they showed up and played with a fury that was most amazing for its consistency; they were physical and they competed and they played every week to win. Players accepted the roles Cowher defined, and then they either stepped up to pick up the slack or stepped back without pouting, depending upon what was needed from them at the time.

The 2004 Steelers would lose the AFC Championship Game, largely because it came on a day when their quarterback finally played like the rookie he was. While

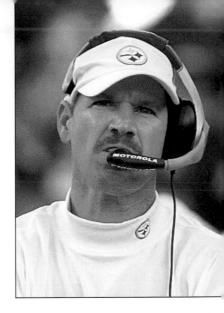

the Steelers were back on track philosophically and had returned to a place among the NFL's elite, Cowher looked at it all and saw only unfinished business. He would say as much two days after that loss to the New England Patriots. "Sometimes we wonder why. Ours is not to wonder why, ours is to continue to try."

The 2005 season was trying, indeed. Ben Roethlisberger took a couple of shots on the knee and ended up missing four games, three of them following an arthroscopic procedure that taught all of Pittsburgh how to spell "meniscus." Then, his right thumb became the most famous opposable digit in TV news history. Hines Ward missed one of the same games Roethlisberger missed. In late November, the Steelers had to play a

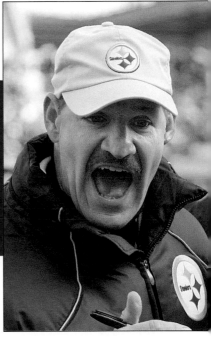

By the time 7-5 had become 11-5, the Steelers were more than just in the playoffs. Thanks to Cowher, they were prepared for the playoffs and the win-or-go-home reality of them.

division game on the road without their Pro Bowl left tackle, their All-Pro inside linebacker and their top two quarterbacks.

When their team was intact, the Steelers were capable of some impressive things, examples being those early wins on the road in San Diego and Cincinnati. Those were instances of the Steelers being more physical, and ultimately more committed to winning, than their opponent, which indicated their mind-set was still re-established.

But they muddled through a lot of it as well. Three straight mid-season wins — over Baltimore, Green Bay and Cleveland teams that would finish a combined 16-32 — were ugly in their own unique ways, but they offered a glimpse of a team still filled with the kind of people willing to step up to pick up the slack or step back without pouting, depending upon what was needed from them at the time.

Teams that win championships always improve during the course of their seasons to a point where they're playing their best when the games count the most, and the real toll the Steelers' injuries took was to slow this process for them. Without Roethlisberger, and then without Marvel Smith to stabilize the offense's ability to protect him, the passing attack atrophied. That became a glaring weakness, and in the NFL glaring weaknesses impact everything on a team.

When the Steelers lost three straight games to bring them to the second week of December with a 7-5 record, and against the backdrop of a mathematical possibility to win out and still miss the playoffs, everybody there was looking for some direction. The only person who could chart the course was Bill Cowher.

It started the day after the third of the defeats, a 38-31 loss to the Bengals that essentially eliminated the Steelers from the AFC North race. Cowher brought the players in and had them watch the video of the game; having each one grade himself on every snap reinforced the concept of the importance of individual accountability. Every man was going to be asked to pick up his game, and Bill Cowher showed them he included himself, too.

Bill Cowher shares a moment during training camp with Director of Football Operations Kevin Colbert, whose contribution Cowher made sure to recognize after the Steelers captured their fifth Super Bowl title.

The next day, Cowher's opening statement at his weekly news conference included: "All the focus this week with our football team is on this football game. I'm not going to speculate on the future or dwell on the past ... We recognize the importance of the game, and where we are, and the fact that we need to stop this three-game slide we're on. That's the state of where we are and the approach we're taking."

And so it was, with a practice in full pads the next day serving as his own unique exclamation point. Cowher never wavered in his message, he never was deterred from his plan, the Steelers got healthy and were able to put together the long-delayed self-improvement portion of their season. By the time 7-5 had become 11-5, the Steelers were more than just in the playoffs. Thanks to Cowher, they were prepared for the playoffs and the win-or-go-home reality of them.

"We have a team that respects one another," Cowher said the week the Steelers would open the playoffs in Cincinnati against the Bengals. "There are a lot of guys who have accepted roles and embraced those roles even though they may want to play more. I think there's an unselfishness that permeated through this team based on the good veteran leadership we've had. That being said, they also understand what it takes this time of year ..."

It took a lot of hard work and commitment from every player and every assistant on Cowher's staff, and he repeatedly acknowledged that along the way. But he also never got off his message — one week at a time, one opponent at a time, one game at a time — even to the point of whispering "one more game" in Dan Rooney's ear on the sideline in Denver as the AFC Championship Game was about to become history.

Bill Cowher had coached the Steelers to the Super Bowl, and the manner in which he personally handled it all was exactly what a leader should do. He gracefully accepted the questions about his past losses in big games, he gave credit to his players and coaches and he showed no interest in stopping them from being the people they are. He thanked the Rooneys, he acknowledged the fans, he took part in the Jerome Bettis Story, and when it came to the football aspect he approached things no differently than he had the week before the Bears game. He was loose, and his only agenda was to win.

When it ended this time with a victory in the last game, Cowher still didn't change. He stood at the podium on Monday morning with his fingerprints all over the Lombardi Trophy, and while he could have made the moment about him, he instead was humble and gracious and thankful. "I said before, in my 14 years in Pittsburgh, we've had good teams, we've had confident teams, but this was the closest team we've ever had ... There are a lot of things that made this group a special group. The coaching staff we had, the best coaching staff, I think, in the National Football League. So I give a lot of credit to them, and it certainly starts at the top with the stability of Mr. (Dan) Rooney and Kevin Colbert."

Yes, the stability and all the good things to be derived from it start at the top, but when it comes time to remember all of the reasons why the 2005 Pittsburgh Steelers won Super Bowl XL, well, that needs to start with the job Bill Cowher did as their coach.

raining Camp

Laying the groundwork

At the end of their 2004 season, the Pittsburgh Steelers looked to be in great shape for the immediate future. Over the course of the previous year, they had gotten back to the style of football that fit them best and no changes to the coaching staff meant continuity there; the roster was packed with players who had starting experience in their systems, or elsewhere in the league, or both; and the simple, inevitable passage of time was going to take care of their starting quarterback being a rookie.

There is no such thing as complete stability in the National Football League, but the losses the Steelers sustained during the offseason portion of 2005 only were seen as significant by sports talk show hosts who had to manufacture something to fill all those hours of airtime, because the NHL strike and bad Major League baseball weren't going to get them through the day.

Keydrick Vincent, the former undrafted rookie who filled in so well at left guard in 2004, got some nice money in free agency from the Baltimore Ravens, but he was going to be replaced by Kendall Simmons, the former No. 1 pick whose torn ACL toward the end of an afternoon practice at training camp had created the opening. Oliver Ross, the journeyman right tackle, cashed in as well with the Arizona Cardinals, but the Steelers had former No. 3 draft pick Max Starks, about to begin his second season, ready to step in there. The only change to the starting defensive unit was an addition — Pro Bowl nose tackle Casey Hampton was coming back after missing the bulk of the regular season with his own torn ACL.

The Plaxico Burress situation was the one fans chose to sink their teeth into, but there truly was no meat there, either. The eighth overall pick of the 2000 NFL draft, Burress at times was a big-play receiver who could take over a game, and at other times he was just another 6-foot-5 guy with inconsistent hands. Burress never was going to be what

his supporters believed he already was, but he wasn't the subversive malcontent his detractors labeled him, either. In the final analysis, what Plaxico Burress was going to cost toward the Steelers salary cap was a number too high for them to pay, and so the team was proactive in moving on to sign unrestricted free agent Cedrick Wilson days before the New York Giants came to terms with Burress.

Kevin Colbert oversaw a draft that yielded the best tight end prospect available, plus depth at cornerback and offensive tackle. It certainly lacked the pizzazz of the previous year's that brought a franchise quarterback in the first round, but a team choosing 30th in every round usually finds that all the pizzazz has been picked over already. It was a nice draft.

The rest of the offseason was similarly "nice" in that guys took part in minicamp and the coaching sessions, and with Burress having signed with the Giants, Mother's Day passed without incident. So tranquil was the Steelers offseason that the two biggest stories of it were Ben Roethlisberger legally riding his Harley-Davidson motorcycle without a helmet,

> *Casey Hampton had been so impressive, in fact, that the Steelers signed him to a contract extension through 2009. "Everybody worried about (Hines Ward)," said Hampton, "and I just snuck in through the back door and got mine done."*

and Myron Cope retiring after 35 years as the color analyst on the team's radio broadcasts. There was no final determination, however, on whether the noise from the Harley or from Cope was found to be more frightening to young children.

Five days before camp was to open at St. Vincent College, Eugene Parker, Hines Ward's agent, spoiled the tranquility when he wouldn't say whether his client was going to report on time. Ward had one year left on a contract extension he had signed days before the 2001 opener, and he had been told that getting him another extension was a priority. Well, there either was a misunderstanding brewing as to what "priority" meant, or there was some old-fashioned posturing going on, because big-time sports agents typically know whether a Pro Bowl client is going to report to training camp on time.

With a different team, a player with a signed contract deciding to hold out for a better deal might not cause much of a ripple, but with the Steelers, well, this was the very issue that festered to the extent

Ten minutes into the news conference announcing Hines Ward's return to the team, all was forgiven by both sides. Ward couldn't wipe the grin off his face because he came away from his talk with Bill Cowher feeling appreciated, and the Steelers now could continue the process of making Ward a very wealthy man.

the team decided to release Franco Harris after four Super Bowls and on the eve of a season when he undoubtedly was going to pass Jim Brown and become the NFL's all-time rushing leader. When 6 p.m. on July 31 passed and Ward was a no-show, the Steelers responded immediately.

"It's always been the policy of this organization that there will be no negotiations while a player who is under contract is not in camp," said Director of Football Operations Kevin Colbert. "We think anybody under contract has an obligation to the team." With that, all negotiations stopped, and if nobody wanted to say it out loud, the simple truth was Ward either was going to acquiesce and report to training camp, or he was going to come to be linked forever with Harris in a negative way.

While the fans took sides and energetically debated the issue to the delight of the talk shows, Coach Bill Cowher and the rest of the team got on with the business at hand. The previous summer had marked one of the most physical and competitive training camps of Cowher's career with the team, and the intensity and focus of this one picked right up where that one left off. The first practice in pads was laced with the kind of intensity and enthusiasm normally reserved for games that count in the standings, and the unusually high number of fans who packed the hills on that sunny Tuesday afternoon roared their approval.

But there is a reason why this period of every summer

is referred to as the "dog days," and what a mutt those days turned out to be for the Steelers. Nothing upsets the flow of a training camp like injuries, and within a week after their own Super Tuesday, the Steelers had lost both Duce Staley and Joey Porter for the rest of the pre-season to arthroscopic knee surgeries. Meanwhile, the Ward situation was threatening to become bitter and personal, and that's when Jerome Bettis made his first big play of 2005.

Bettis was the guy who had taken back-to-back pay cuts because he couldn't envision himself playing for a team other than the Steelers, he was the guy who had welcomed Staley to the team the year before even though it was obvious he had been signed to be the starting running back, and he was the guy for whom so many had shed tears following that loss to the New England Patriots in the 2004 AFC Championship Game. This situation with Ward needed mediation, but it had to be by someone who was respected by both sides of the dispute. Bettis was the only man for the job.

It was Bettis who convinced Ward to make the move to call Bill Cowher, to talk things out, to re-open the lines of communication. And then Cowher took it from there. Ward needed to know he was valued, he needed to hear he was important to the team's present and its future, and unless all that came from the head coach it was just going to be lip service. Cowher told Ward the truth, which also happened to be what he wanted to hear, and within a short time the sides decided that a news conference 90 minutes before the nationally tele-

vised preseason opener would be perfect to announce Ward's decision to report to camp.

Ten minutes into Ward's news conference, all was forgiven by both sides. Ward couldn't wipe the grin off his face because he came away from his talk with Cowher feeling appreciated, and the Steelers now could continue the process of making Ward a very wealthy man. But the football reality was that this foolishness had retarded the growth of the team's passing attack, and as the Steelers began the final portion of their 2005 training camp they were still quite rough around the edges.

With Porter targeting the regular season opener for his return, it became obvious that James Harrison and Clark Haggans were the only other competent outside linebackers on the roster. The offensive line wasn't real solid yet, and that's not so big a deal until the preseason games start and the quarterbacks start getting hit.

The glass-half-full version pointed to the three young cornerbacks competing to replace 35-year-old Willie Williams, with Ike Taylor being the most consistently impressive by far; sixth-round pick Chris Kemoeatu showed himself to be an aggressive, athletic guard; and

The Steelers closed the 2005 preseason with running back Duce Staley, linebacker Joey Porter and running back Jerome Bettis all sidelined because of injuries.

Casey Hampton and Kendall Simmons both looked to have gotten back to their pre-injury forms. Hampton had been so impressive, in fact, that the Steelers signed him to a contract extension through 2009. "Everybody worried about (Ward)," said Hampton, "and I just snuck in through the back door and got mine done."

Less than 24 hours after camp broke and the Steelers escaped St. Vincent College, Bettis injured a calf muscle in a preseason game against the Washington Redskins. "If Jerome is unable to go," said Cowher at the time, "Willie Parker will start." He was talking about the season opener on Sept. 11 against the Tennessee Titans, not the third of four preseason games.

The Steelers concluded a 3-1 preseason by beating Carolina, and then getting the contract extension done with Ward a few days after, but those bits of good news didn't have much to do with the team being ready for the start of the regular season.

"I like this group of guys, but we are nowhere where we need to be right now," said Cowher, who would later add, "Would I like to see us more in sync in the passing game? Yes."

Regular Season

Good start, great finish

"It's like the first day of school. You're ready to go back, everything's on the line. I mean, everything counts now. Preseason is kind of hard to get up for. You're back and playing football, but nothing counts. But the opener is the first excitement. Everyone in the league has the same record, and everyone's goal is to win the Super Bowl."

— Hines Ward

"I feel good about the guys. What's going to happen this season? It's hard to say. We have yet to be defined. We're still growing as a football team. We're still evolving. We're still trying to create that chemistry. You just don't walk into a season with an identity. It's like respect, you have to earn it. That's not something handed to you because you played well the year before. It's going to be a process, and it's going to be a grind, and it's going to be challenging. If our guys understand that, take an unselfish approach to it, keep things in perspective, then we have a chance."

— Coach Bill Cowher

For the previous six months, the Steelers had been under a microscope. Every team in every NFL city had been under a microscope, because that's what the offseason had become. Because the league's calendar had free agency follow the season closely, and then the draft came during the latter part of free agency, and then minicamps and coaching sessions happened right after that, and then training camps opened a month after that, NFL teams were in the news constantly.

Professional sports is a scoreboard business, however, and because the NFL doesn't turn on the scoreboards for real until the start of the regular season, it's very difficult for fans to quantify progress or lack thereof, but it doesn't mean they stop trying to do just that. By the time a team is finished with its training camp, every wart has been exposed, every scab has been picked until it bleeds. But what's always missing during this process is perspective, because in a scoreboard business the team with more points is declared a

winner regardless of the weaknesses it may have brought into the game.

As the 2005 regular season was about to begin, the Pittsburgh Steelers were thin at running back because their two veterans both were rehabilitating leg injuries; their passing attack had no rhythm; two of their top three outside linebackers were nursing injuries and they

had no legitimate No. 4. The first-team offense hadn't produced a touchdown in four preseason games, and the defense was allowing opponents to complete more than 60 percent of their passes.

Each one of those observations was verifiable, but the reality of the NFL in September 2005 was that there were many, many teams in far worse shape. The Steelers didn't have to dip very far into their schedule to find a couple of examples, and once those games against Tennessee and Houston were over, they were 2-0 and being talked about in the most glowing of terms, even though they still were pretty much the same team that was being judged to be so deficient.

The pass offense that was borderline incompetent throughout the preseason was nearly perfect in eight quarters against the Titans and Texans. Willie Parker went from a guy who couldn't get on the field for a 2-10 University of North Carolina team to a Gale Sayers look-alike, with back-to-back 100-yard games that included runs of 45, 25, 19 and 15 yards. The defense had 11 sacks already and had allowed just two touchdowns, one in the first quarter of the opener and one after it already was 20-0 in the second game.

But the most amazing aspect of these early 2005 games, just as it seemed to be during every week of the previous season, was the play of Ben Roethlisberger. The notion of a sophomore slump for Roethlisberger was debatable on its surface, because quarterbacks typically improve markedly with experience, but it also seemed inevitable that a guy who was fifth in the NFL in passer rating, second in yards per attempt, tied for fourth in completion percentage and 13-0 as a starter as a rookie would experience some drop-off, because how much better could it get?

Yet it did get better. In those two games, the second of which he played after missing almost an entire week of practice with a sore knee, Roethlisberger completed 72 percent of his passes for a ridiculously high 14.75 yards per attempt, with four touchdowns and no interceptions. Analysts kept cautioning that Roethlisberger couldn't be judged completely until he was part of an offense requiring him to attempt 30-plus passes in every game, but what truly was amazing about this 23-year-old was his ability to be incredibly productive with relatively few opportunities.

At 2-0, the Steelers were headed for another go-around with the New England Patriots, and there was a faction believing that this was much more than just the third regular season game of 16 on the schedule. Twice in the previous four years the Patriots had ended the Steelers' season in the conference championship game, and both times that had happened in Pittsburgh. Bill Cowher was cast as Ahab to Bill Belichick's great white whale, and the Patriots were seen as the first 2005 opponent capable of revealing what kind of team these Steelers actually were.

The Patriots would win on a last-second field goal by Adam Vinatieri in a game that was every bit as close as the 23-20 final score indicated, but the reaction in Pittsburgh was some morose combination of gloom and surrender. Largely ignored were the false start penalty that erased a 47-yard field goal by Jeff Reed and the ill-advised lateral from Antwaan Randle El that became a turnover deep in Patriots territory; instead, the fandom preferred to view the outcome as another example of

Cowher being outcoached by Belichick. At their bye, the Steelers were 2-1, but their one loss was seen as evidence that not enough had changed, that they again lacked the necessary stuff to win a championship because they were unable to dethrone the defending champions.

That kind of attitude would have been fatal had it infected a team with 13 more games to play, and Cowher started hammering his own message home immediately. "We'll bounce back from this. We have to. There are a lot of things we can learn from this game, and we will. We'll recognize that we have a tough schedule ahead of us, and we'll just take it one at a time." Coachspeak, sure, but what other options were there? Capitulation in late September? Ridiculous.

> *The win over the Chargers on that emotionally charged night in San Diego spoke volumes about the Steelers.*

By the end of 2005, the Steelers would be a team that loved long odds, that thrived in situations where things apparently were working against them, that loved it most when it was "us against the world." Losing to the Patriots stirred all of that up again, and when upcoming opponent San Diego thrashed New England, 41-17, in Foxboro the same weekend the Steelers were off, well, the outcome of Monday, Oct. 10 seemed to be a foregone conclusion.

The win over the Chargers on that emotionally charged night in San Diego spoke volumes about the Steelers, and it was an accomplishment the players and coaches really could build upon. Coming off that rout of the Patriots, the Chargers were considered a hot team even though they were 2-2 because their losses to Dallas and at Denver had been by seven points combined. Their offense had scored 86 points in the previous two games, and the San Diego defense was a physical one that did not give up rushing yards easily.

The Steelers went to Southern California and weathered the early frenzy naturally associated with the area's first Monday night game in over a decade, and then they got down and slugged it out with the Chargers on the way to a 14-7 halftime lead. San Diego's offense was hot to start the third quarter, and on three straight possessions it ran a total of 21 plays for 154 yards, but at the opportune moment on each drive the Steelers defense rose up and made a play to force a field goal. Trailing 16-14, the Steelers offense then gave the rest of the league a little preview of what was to come, and whichever teams were paying attention could not have been pleased with what they saw.

After a 37-yard kickoff return put the ball at the Steelers 38-yard line, Roethlisberger took over. The first play was a 33-yard pass to Hines Ward; the second a 13-yard pass to Ward; and then when the Chargers assumed this second-year quarterback was locked on to his Pro Bowl receiver, Roethlisberger moved the safety with a pump fake and

The Bears came to Heinz Field on Dec. 11 with the league's top-ranked defense, but it was the Steelers who had the best defense that day. One example was Clark Haggans' sack of rookie quarterback Kyle Orton.

connected with tight end Heath Miller over the middle for a 16-yard touchdown. Seventy-one seconds from start to finish, and the Steelers were back in the lead, 21-16.

The Chargers would score a touchdown to take a 22-21 lead, and in the process of putting together the game-winning drive, Roethlisberger got hit on the knee by Luis Castillo while throwing a 9-yard pass to Antwaan Randle El, and that injury would sideline him and thus precipitate the giveaway loss to Jacksonville the following Sunday. As Jeff Reed's 40-yard field goal soared between the uprights to make Pittsburgh a 24-22 winner and put all of San Diego in a funk, the Steelers had crossed over and become another one of those teams with an indispensable quarterback.

Roethlisberger was back for the game in Cincinnati on Oct. 23, and that loss to the Jaguars had created another of those do-or-die situations for the Steelers. With a record crowd packed into Paul Brown Stadium, the Steelers did to the Bengals what teachers used to do to misbehaving children once upon a time. During the second half of their 27-13 win, the Steelers outscored the Bengals 20-7, and they did it with 32 running plays and only six passes. Forget the standings, the Steelers, even at 4-2, still were in charge of the AFC North.

Six weeks later, the Steelers would drop the rematch to the Bengals to conclude a three-game losing streak

and all but mathematically eliminate themselves from the division race, and it was telling that the way they lost to Cincinnati was the exact opposite of the way they had played in the win. Four turnovers, including three interceptions by Roethlisberger in 41 attempts, hurt them badly, but the fact he also passed for 386 yards and three touchdowns showed the coaching staff he could do damage to opponents through the air. The Steelers were 7-5 after the Bengals left town, but they also were getting closer to being a very dangerous opponent even as they were putting themselves in a position where they needed help to get into the playoffs.

The Chicago Bears came to Heinz Field on Dec. 11 riding an eight-game winning streak and they showed up with one of the league's top-ranked defenses, a unit powered by a ferocious front seven. The weather that day was fitting for a December football game between teams from Pittsburgh and Chicago, and maybe that was Mother Nature's way of getting the Steelers back to their offensive identity. Jerome Bettis had 16 carries for 100 yards and a touchdown in the second half, and on his game-clinching score the Bus left All-Pro linebacker Brian Urlacher for road kill. In San Diego, the Chargers lost to Miami, and the Steelers had gotten the help they needed. Now, it was going to be up to them.

The following week, the Steelers used defense and special teams to dominate the Vikings, 18-3, in Minnesota; on Christmas Eve, they traveled to Cleveland and grinched the Browns, 41-0; and then they celebrated New Year's Day with a playoff-clinching 35-21 win over Detroit.

The NFL playoffs were set to begin, and one month after their chances were on life support, the Steelers were in the tournament, and the most telling thing about it was they didn't view that alone as an accomplishment.

"It's not about getting into the playoffs, or getting past the first round. That's just the first step," said Jeff Hartings. "When you're thinking about the goals we have ... right now all we care about is the next team."

The 2005 playoffs had arrived, and the Steelers had earned the identity they would carry into them.

Game 1

TENNESSEE	7
PITTSBURGH	34

Date: Sept. 11
Site: Heinz Field
Weather conditions:
75 degrees, sunny

Steelers leaders
Rushing: Willie Parker, 22 carries for 161 yards, 1 TD
Passing: Ben Roethlisberger, 9-for-11 for 218 yards, 2 TD, 0 INT
Receiving: Antwaan Randle El, 2 catches for 89 yards, 1 TD
Defense: LB Joey Porter, 4 tackles, 1 sack, 1 forced fumble

Key moment: The score was tied 7-7 early in the second quarter when Tennessee running back Travis Henry fumbled and Ike Taylor recovered at the Titans 48-yard line. The Steelers converted the turnover into a field goal and after holding the Titans to one first down Roethlisberger hit Randle El with a 63-yard touchdown pass that opened up a 10-point lead.

Steelers Digest Player of the Week:
RB Willie Parker

Quote to remember:
"I guess a lot of y'all got your questions answered, asking me, can I last the whole game? I mean, I should ask y'all the question now."

— Parker

Antwaan Randle El's 63-yard touchdown reception late in the second quarter helped extend the Steelers' lead to 17-7.

The Steelers' first offensive possession of the 2005 regular season ended with rookie tight end Heath Miller's 3-yard touchdown reception.

Running back Willie Parker answered the call in his first start with the Steelers by rushing for 161 yards on 22 carries.

From the Pages of
Steelers Digest

Combine perfect quarterback play with a running attack that rolled up over 200 yards; starter Willie Parker accounted for 161, and his average of 7.3 per carry is just not the way it's typically done in the NFL. They had no turnovers; the offensive line allowed no sacks; and there were only two penalties, one of which was nothing but a speed bump on a touchdown drive, and all the other did was prevent a little overkill.

It was a grand afternoon, indeed, and for the record Coach Bill Cowher was the first guy to wrap the whole afternoon in a wet blanket. Yes, that's his job, but, yes, he's right as well.

— By Bob Labriola

I don't think we played a very crisp game, to be honest with you. We didn't start off very fast at all. We missed some blocks on offense and gave up some big passes and big plays on defense. We didn't tackle real well at the beginning of the game.

We played hard as a team; we did not beat ourselves; and I like that part of it. We didn't have any turnovers or unforced penalties.

For the most part, it was a solid effort, but we still have a long way to go.

— Coach Bill Cowher

Things turned out OK, but they didn't start real well for the Steelers defense. The Titans received the opening kickoff and drove 61 yards on 11 plays for a touchdown. Steve McNair completed 4 of 5 passes, including one for the 1-yard touchdown.

Of McNair's 18 completions for 219 yards, 11 of them for 108 yards went to the tight ends.

But what the defense did was make big plays to end Titans possessions. Troy Polamalu's interception and Chris Hope's fumble recovery both came in the red zone.

— Game reports

Third-down back Verron Haynes celebrates his third-quarter 5-yard touchdown run, which closed out the scoring.

Game 2

PITTSBURGH	27
HOUSTON	7

Date: Sept. 18
Site: Reliant Stadium
Weather conditions: 90 degrees, 57 percent humidity

Steelers leaders
Rushing: Willie Parker, 25 carries for 111 yards, 1 TD
Passing: Ben Roethlisberger, 14-for-21 for 254 yards, 2 TD, 0 INT
Receiving: Hines Ward, 6 catches for 84 yards, 2 TD
Defense: S Troy Polamalu, 6 tackles, 3 sacks, 1 pass defensed

Key moment: After the Steelers marched to a field goal on the opening possession of the game, the defense quickly established its dominance. Clark Haggans sacked David Carr on third down and forced a fumble that was recovered by Joey Porter. The turnover set up a Ward touchdown that made the score 10-0.

Steelers Digest Player of the Week: QB Ben Roethlisberger

Quote to remember:
"He's our starter. I don't think you need to keep asking me that. I gotta keep other guys involved and I'll attempt to do that, but Willie Parker's going nowhere."
— **Coach Bill Cowher**

Willie Parker followed up his sensational debut in Week 1 by rushing for 111 yards, including this 10-yard touchdown in the third quarter.

Quarterback Ben Roethlisberger had his second consecutive game with two touchdown passes and no interceptions.

Hines Ward's two touchdown receptions in the first half gave the Steelers all the scoring they would need against the Texans.

Safety Troy Polamalu led the all-out assault against Houston quarterback David Carr by recording three of the team's eight sacks.

Troy Polamalu gets the first game ball for his three sacks, the biggest of which took the Texans out of field goal range late in the first half.

The second goes to Casey Hampton, who had tons of fun in his homecoming. Hampton made only three tackles, but he blew up several plays before they got started. I've asked Hampton if the heat bothers him during the training camp run-test.

He always laughs and says, "This is cold where I come from."
— **By Jim Wexell**

If there looked to be a week when Ben Roethlisberger was going to struggle, this appeared to be it. Just the second week of the season, Roethlisberger missed two days of practice with an injury, and the decision to start him wasn't made until the day of the game.

Whatever effects might have lingered with respect to the bone bruise in his knee were not apparent in the opening possession, or later. He moved freely in the pocket to buy time, and his passes were largely on target.

On one third-down situation in the third quarter, Roethlisberger rolled to his right until he was outside the numbers painted on the turf, and then he turned and threw the ball 40 yards downfield to Cedrick Wilson, who was outside the numbers on the opposite side of the field.
— **By Bob Labriola**

Starting fast takes the crowd out of it. Also, playing smart, not turning the football over and no foolish penalties. You try to take away the big play. If you can do that, the crowd never gets into it. You talk about playing on the road and starting fast and playing smart. If you feed off the crowd, it becomes us against them, an us-against-the-world type of thing.
— **Coach Bill Cowher**

Game 3

NEW ENGLAND 23
PITTSBURGH 20

Date: Sept. 25
Site: Heinz Field
Weather conditions:
83 degrees, partly cloudy

Steelers leaders
Rushing: Willie Parker, 17 carries for 55 yards
Passing: Ben Roethlisberger, 12-for-28 for 216 yards, 2 TD, 0 INT
Receiving: Hines Ward, 4 catches for 110 yards, 2 TD
Defense: LB Clark Haggans, 12 tackles, 1 sack, 2 forced fumbles

Key moment: After the Steelers tied the score with 1:21 left, New England began its last drive at its 38-yard line with no timeouts left. But Tom Brady completions of 17 and 14 yards to running backs Kevin Faulk and Patrick Pass immediately put the Patriots in range for the game-winning field goal.

Steelers Digest Player of the Week:
LB Clark Haggans

Quote to remember:
"It's like basketball; we were playing for the last shot. If we make (the field goal), we make it. If not, then it's overtime. We didn't want to have something happen to get us out of field goal range."
— New England coach Bill Belichick

Hines Ward races away from a couple of New England defenders on his way to an 85-yard touchdown, which would be the Steelers' longest offensive play of the season.

The New England pass rush gave the Steelers problems, with defensive tackle Richard Seymour bringing down Ben Roethlisberger twice.

It seemed like we couldn't get any consistent running game going, and we had a lot of minus-plays. It seemed like Ben got sacked a lot of times. We were in some third-and-long situations. It seemed like we were playing backed up most of the game. We really couldn't get a whole lot going offensively, and credit their defense.

— Coach Bill Cowher

With the Steelers, it's not all about Ben Roethlisberger just yet, but everybody knows you're not going to have any chance to defeat the defending champs without good quarterback play. With the Patriots, it's always going to be all about Tom Brady, because just in case those two Super Bowl MVP trophies aren't enough evidence of his indispensability, pop in the video of last Sunday's game at Heinz Field.

To say that Brady was the difference in the Patriots' last-second 23-20 win over the Steelers would be true, but it also would not be poetic enough to describe his impact on one of the most entertaining games of this young NFL season.

In the football vernacular, it's called "making plays," but what Brady was doing in real life was a lot more complicated.

— By Bob Labriola

Barrett Brooks was flagged for a false start on a 47-yard field goal attempt by Jeff Reed that was good. After the penalty, Reed was wide left from 52 yards, which ended his streak at 22 in a row.

Ricardo Colclough returned a kickoff 44 yards to give the Steelers good field position for the tying touchdown drive, but Ellis Hobbs returned Reed's kickoff 34 yards to put Tom Brady in good position (for the game-winning drive).

— Game reports

Linebacker Larry Foote runs downfield after recovering a New England fumble, one of the defense's three takeaways on the day.

The Steelers try in vain to block the last-second Adam Vinatieri kick that would become the game-winning 43-yard field goal.

Game 4

PITTSBURGH 24
SAN DIEGO 22

Date: Oct. 10
Site: Qualcomm Stadium
Weather conditions:
64 degrees, clear

Steelers leaders
Rushing: Jerome Bettis,
17 carries for 54 yards, 1 TD
Passing: Ben Roethlisberger, 17-
for-26 for 225 yards, 1 TD, 0 INT
Receiving: Hines Ward,
6 catches for 83 yards
Defense: LB James Farrior,
8 tackles

Key moment: Roethlisberger
was marvelous on the final drive,
but what allowed the Steelers to
make it a game-winning drive
was the defense's ability to stop
LaDainian Tomlinson on a
two-point conversion attempt
after San Diego had scored a
touchdown to take a 22-21 lead.

**Steelers Digest
Player of the Week:**
QB Ben Roethlisberger

Quote to remember:
*"For the most part, we moved
the ball up and down the field in
the second half. We just didn't
make enough plays."*
**— San Diego coach
Marty Schottenheimer**

Offensive tackle
Max Starks gives
kicker Jeff Reed a lift
after Reed's 40-yard
field goal in the
waning seconds gave
the Steelers a
statement victory
at San Diego.

Linebacker James Harrison went airborne while returning a first-half interception.

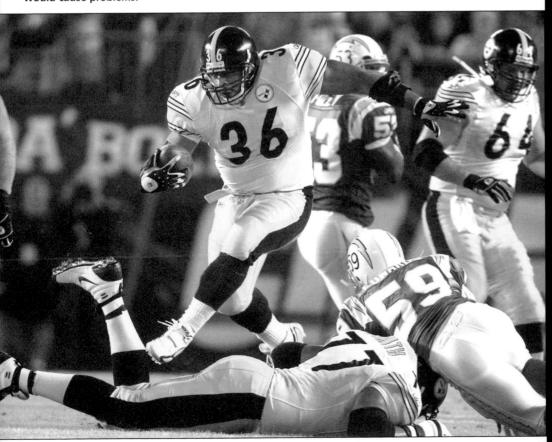

Ben Roethlisberger took some hits against the Chargers, including a shot to the knee that eventually would cause problems.

Jerome Bettis saw his first action of the season at San Diego, rushing for 54 yards and a second-quarter touchdown.

This is what good teams do. They come to places like this and beat opponents like this on a stage like this. And they do it by overcoming officials and injuries and whatever else might come into play ...

A fortnight ago, the Pittsburgh Steelers were considered a good team, pretty much by acclamation ... But then came a loss to New England, and apparently, Armageddon. What they did to a Chargers team that was among the hottest in the league should pull the plug on a lot of that.

The Steelers' 24-22 win over the Chargers doesn't mean any more, in truth, than the loss to the Patriots ... but this is the kind of win that reveals a team's mettle, and it's now apparent that these Steelers have what it's going to take to contend for a championship this season.

— By Bob Labriola

"From an offensive standpoint, we've been really good at getting down there and scoring touchdowns. But tonight, even though we got inside their 30-yard line six times, we only got two touchdowns and three field goals, instead of scoring touchdowns in that situation 80 percent of the time, like we had been."

— Chargers QB Drew Brees

Aided either by penalties on the Steelers or big gains that came after the initial play broke down, the Chargers put together three field goal drives to take a 16-14 lead with 11:41 left in the game. But on each of those drives, the Steelers defense made a play to hold San Diego to only three points.

— Game reports

The Steelers, of course, belong in the top tier of the mighty AFC with the Patriots, Colts and Chargers. I don't know enough about the Broncos yet. Nobody does.

— By Jim Wexell

Game 5

JACKSONVILLE 23
PITTSBURGH 17

Date: Oct. 16
Site: Heinz Field
Weather conditions:
56 degrees, partly cloudy

Steelers leaders
Rushing: Willie Parker,
21 carries for 55 yards
Passing: Tommy Maddox, 11-for-28 for 154 yards, 1 TD, 3 INT
Receiving: Heath Miller,
4 catches for 72 yards, 1 TD
Defense: CB Ike Taylor, 5 tackles,
2 passes defensed

Key moment: It was bad enough when Maddox fumbled the snap on third-and-11 from the Jacksonville 27-yard line on the first drive of overtime to kill a game-winning field goal opportunity, but then Maddox was picked off by Rashean Mathis, who returned the interception 41 yards for the game-winning TD.

Steelers Digest Player of the Week:
CB Ike Taylor

Quote to remember:
"Putting everything else aside, the kickoff return (to open overtime) gave us a great chance to win the game. And we just kind of blundered it and didn't even give ourselves a chance."
— C Jeff Hartings

Joey Porter forced a fumble when he sacked Byron Leftwich in the second quarter, but the Steelers weren't able to recover the loose ball.

Antwaan Randle El gave the Steelers a 14-7 lead in the second quarter when he returned a punt 72 yards for a touchdown, but the Steelers wouldn't reach the end zone again on this day.

Tommy Maddox (8) can only look on in dejection after his fumble in Jacksonville territory early in the overtime killed a potential game-winning scoring opportunity.

When you turn the football over four times and are minus-3 in turnover ratio, you aren't going to win many football games. We had the opportunity, even in overtime. It's very frustrating, at this point, walking away with a defeat.

— **Coach Bill Cowher**

A 74-yard kickoff return by Quincy Morgan put the ball at the Jaguars 26-yard line to open overtime. Last week in a similar spot on the field and needing a field goal to win, Jerome Bettis pounded the ball and then Jeff Reed kicked the game-winner. This time, Willie Parker was the running back. He carried twice for minus-1 yard, and on third down Tommy Maddox fumbled the exchange from center and the Jaguars recovered at their own 36-yard line.

— **Game reports**

For a team that's not all about the quarterback, a team that likes not being all about the quarterback, it sure was all about the quarterback ...

... In between the time Ben Roethlisberger's knee got torpedoed in San Diego and the moment Coach Bill Cowher announced Tommy Maddox as the starter, people debated the issue and supported their favorite as if it were politics ...

During the week leading up to this game, Cowher talked about the importance of the Steelers taking care of business against the Jaguars or facing the reality of negating what they accomplished in San Diego against a defending division champion on the road. The loss to the Jaguars did that. It negated that wonderful Monday night in San Diego.

It also did something else. It exposed the Steelers as another team that, in fact, is all about the quarterback.

And that quarterback's name is Ben Roethlisberger.

— **By Bob Labriola**

Game 6

PITTSBURGH	**27**
CINCINNATI	**13**

Date: Oct. 23
Site: Paul Brown Stadium
Weather conditions:
47 degrees, rain

Steelers leaders
Rushing: Willie Parker, 18 carries
for 131 yards, 1 TD
Passing: Ben Roethlisberger, 9-
for-14 for 93 yards, 2 TD, 1 INT
Receiving: Heath Miller,
6 catches for 58 yards, 1 TD
Defense: S Chris Hope,
6 tackles, 1 interception

Key moment: The Steelers led
only 7-6 in the third quarter
before the defense went to work
on Carson Palmer. Hope's
interception, which he returned
55 yards, set up a field goal.
On the next series, Aaron Smith
picked off Palmer at the line of
scrimmage, setting up Parker's
37-yard touchdown run that
made it 17-6.

**Steelers Digest
Player of the Week:**
Offensive line

Quote to remember:
*"We left everything out on the
field today. Guys went hard and
understood how important the
game was. It was one of those
games that we worked for all
week in practice. We all played
for the guy next to you."*
— LB Joey Porter

Thanks to some tremendous blocking by the offensive line as well as fullback Dan Kreider (35), the Steelers were able to rush for 221 yards against the Bengals.

This Heath Miller touchdown catch in the second quarter gave the Steelers a 7-3 lead, and they would never trail again in this game.

Travis Kirschke (90) and Aaron Smith (91) helped the Steelers defensive line make life miserable for Bengals quarterback Carson Palmer.

From the Pages of
Steelers Digest

The coaching staff did a great job rotating the running backs against the Bengals. Just when it became reasonable that Jerome Bettis be the primary ball carrier, Willie Parker ripped off a 37-yard touchdown run around right end. It was the play that broke the game open.

Bettis didn't have a game-turning play, but he had a game-turning series. Bettis entered at the start of the second quarter, and the energy spread through the offense as it did in San Diego. With the Bengals focused on Bettis, Heath Miller came wide open for the play-action touchdown pass.

— By Jim Wexell

"On a serious note, he's very good. Let me stop playing; Ike Taylor is very good. I came into the game thinking it would be very easy, to tell you the truth. And he made me go into my bag of tricks, which is a good thing for the opponent. Therefore, he's in a class of his own."

— Bengals WR Chad Johnson

The Bengals drove deep into Steelers territory on the opening possession, but they ended up with nothing to show for it.

Coach Bill Cowher successfully challenged what was ruled on the field to be a touchdown catch by Chad Johnson; a couple of plays later, Chris Henry dropped a pass in the end zone; and on third down, pressure from Aaron Smith forced Carson Palmer to throw incomplete.

Shayne Graham then yanked a 30-yard field goal attempt wide left.

— Game reports

They knew we were going to run it. Even in the second half, when we knew we were going to run it, the offensive line stepped up. I can't give enough credit to the offensive line and their performance today.

— Coach Bill Cowher

Safety Chris Hope's 55-yard return after a third-quarter interception helped set up a field goal that increased the Steelers' lead to 10-6.

Game 7

BALTIMORE	**19**
PITTSBURGH	**20**

Date: Oct. 31
Site: Heinz Field
Weather conditions:
54 degrees, clear

Steelers leaders
Rushing: Willie Parker, 14 carries
for 63 yards
Passing: Ben Roethlisberger, 18-
for-30 for 177 yards, 2 TD, 1 INT
Receiving: Hines Ward,
8 catches for 75 yards
Defense: S Troy Polamalu,
10 tackles

Key moment: After Jeff Reed's
field goal gave the Steelers a
20-19 lead with 1:36 left, backup
quarterback Anthony Wright
drove Baltimore to midfield until
Brett Keisel came up with
a key sack on third-and-3.
An incompletion on fourth
down clinched the victory.

**Steelers Digest
Player of the Week:**
TE Heath Miller (2 TD catches)

Quote to remember:
*"I think you can take a game like
this and carry it on down the
road, knowing that you can play
better, that you're in a dog fight.
It's just a great win for us. To beat
Baltimore, to win at home — it's
been a long time since we won at
home. It's always a plus to do
that."*

— WR Hines Ward

Longtime Steelers radio voice
Myron Cope was honored during a halftime ceremony that
brought the Terrible Towels out
in full force.

Jeff Reed played the role of hero for the second time in four games, making a game-winning 37-yard field goal with 1:36 left in the fourth quarter.

Tight end Heath Miller provided most of the offense for the Steelers with two touchdown receptions, including this 8-yarder in the third quarter.

The game, well, the game sure looked like it would be a delicious matchup when the league's schedule came out. Sixty minutes of who-can-hit-hardest to determine, at the midway point, which team is the division bully. That's why team president Art Rooney II picked it to be Myron Cope Night in the first place. But as it looks today, the Ravens-as-contenders was spectacularly overrated.

— **By Bob Labriola**

Coach Bill Cowher talked about coming out for this game with a greater energy and focus than the team had in its two previous home games, both losses. The Steelers gave him what he wanted in an opening possession that covered 79 yards in 15 plays and ate up almost nine minutes, only to end with a 4-yard touchdown pass to Heath Miller.

Whatever momentum was established by the offense scoring on the opening possession was handed back when the Ravens drove 73 yards on nine plays to tie the game, 7-7.

On a third-and-12, the Steelers got no pressure on Anthony Wright, who finally dumped the ball off to RB Chester Taylor, who was all alone at the 10-yard line and just got inside the pylon for the touchdown.

— **Game reports**

The coaching staff spent the week selling the potential of the Baltimore Ravens to the players, and they bought it. The Steelers were so tight you would have thought it was a playoff game.

The tightest of all was quarterback Ben Roethlisberger, who missed a wide open Heath Miller running free down the middle on the first play of the game. He didn't come out of the jittery funk but for a brief spell in the third quarter, and for that beautiful last-drive pass to Quincy Morgan.

— **By Jim Wexell**

Game 8

PITTSBURGH	20
GREEN BAY	10

Date: Nov. 6
Site: Lambeau Field
Weather conditions:
49 degrees, partly sunny

Steelers leaders
Rushing: Duce Staley, 15 carries
for 76 yards, 1 TD
Passing: Charlie Batch, 9-for-16
for 65 yards, 0 TD, 1 INT
Receiving: Dan Kreider,
2 catches for 13 yards
Defense: S Troy Polamalu, 6
tackles, 2 fumble recoveries
(one returned 77 yards for a TD)

Key moment: The Steelers
were holding on to a three-point
lead midway through the fourth
quarter when safety Tyrone
Carter picked off Brett Favre
deep in Green Bay territory,
setting up the Staley touchdown
that put the game away.

**Steelers Digest
Player of the Week:**
RB Duce Staley

Quote to remember:
*"I think it is a very big win to
come into this place and beat
that football team. You knew their
backs were against the wall, and
I thought we got off to a good
start. It wasn't pretty football, I
know. But they made enough
plays to win the football game,
and that is the bottom line."*
— Coach Bill Cowher

Safety Troy Polamalu scored the first touchdown of the game when he returned a fumble 77 yards in the second quarter.

Polamalu's touchdown was made possible by cornerback Bryant McFadden, who sacked Brett Favre and caused a fumble on a third-and-goal from the Steelers 12-yard line.

Duce Staley put the game away midway through the fourth quarter with his first touchdown of the season, a 3-yard run that followed a Tyrone Carter interception.

The defense shut down Green Bay running back Samkon Gado, although linebacker James Farrior paid a price on this play when he injured his left knee.

I was happy for Duce. Obviously, that was his first live contact since last year's championship game. He has been running well in practice the last couple of weeks, and he has just been a trooper. He sat there and was very patient and has exemplified the unselfishness that has permeated this football team.

He came in when we needed him, because Willie Parker went down with an ankle injury in the second half, and Duce ran really hard against a pretty good football team.

— Coach Bill Cowher

The Steelers' 20-10 win was a lot of things. It was ugly, and it was against a bad team that did a lot to help them. It was a win attained with the kind of passing attack that wouldn't be good enough in a high school game. But it also was a win achieved without their starting quarterback, without their top two running backs, without their All-Pro inside linebacker.

It was not only a team win for the Steelers, but it was the kind of win that validates the way they construct their team.

— By Bob Labriola

"If someone goes down, someone has to step in and someone has to step up," said Clark Haggans. "Clint (Kriewaldt) is going to step in there, and we're going to keep playing football."

This is an approach that has worked out to the tune of 6-2 for the Steelers at the season's halfway point. James Farrior will join wide receiver Hines Ward, quarterback Ben Roethlisberger, Haggans and cornerback Deshea Townsend on the list of Steelers who have missed starts due to injury.

"We'll go in with the same approach," said Haggans. "Good teams need to have a lot of depth, and we're 6-2 right now."

— By Mike Prisuta

Game 9

CLEVELAND 21
PITTSBURGH 34

Date: Nov. 13
Site: Heinz Field
Weather conditions:
58 degrees, overcast

Steelers leaders
Rushing: Duce Staley, 17 carries for 64 yards
Passing: Charlie Batch, 13-for-19 for 150 yards, 0 TD, 0 INT
Receiving: Hines Ward, 8 catches for 124 yards, 1 TD
Defense: LB Joey Porter, 2 tackles, 1 sack, 1 interception

Key moment: The Steelers took a 10-7 lead against the pesky Browns late in the second quarter, and were able to pad their lead before halftime after Porter intercepted Trent Dilfer. With no timeouts left and time running down, Batch followed a completion to Ward to the 1-yard line with a quarterback sneak for a touchdown.

Steelers Digest Player of the Week:
QB Charlie Batch

Quote to remember:
"Offensively we knew that we were going to have to throw the football. They've been stacking (the box) and we wanted to loosen them up a little bit. We came out and made some big plays."
— Coach Bill Cowher

Before he broke a bone in his right hand, quarterback Charlie Batch turned in a tremendous performance in his second start of the season.

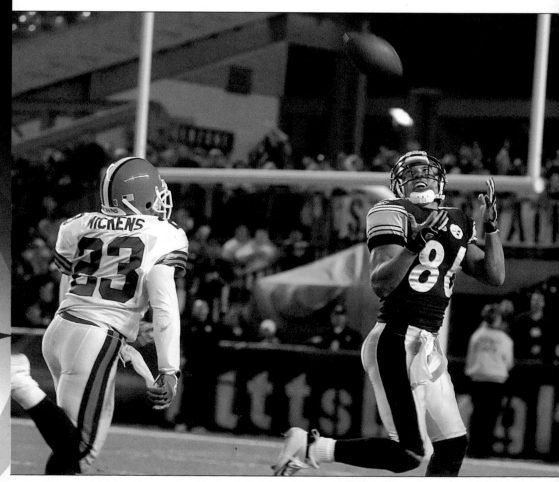

On the same night he became the Steelers' all-time leader in receptions, Hines Ward also caught this 51-yard touchdown pass from fellow wide receiver Antwaan Randle El.

Watching the Steelers beat Cleveland made it a little easier for Ben Roethlisberger to have to sit out a second consecutive game after undergoing arthroscopic knee surgery.

Hines Ward came into the game needing three catches to pass John Stallworth as the team's all-time leading receiver. A 15-yard pass from Charlie Batch to Ward was the 538th catch of his career, and it not only was good for the record but it also put the Steelers in position for the Jeff Reed field goal that gave them a 10-7 lead.

Batch showed good poise as the Steelers raced the first-half clock to score the touchdown that gave them a 17-7 lead. With no timeouts left, Batch completed a pass to Ward, and he was ruled down at the Browns 1-yard line. With nine seconds left and the clock running, Batch hustled the offense to the line and sneaked over the right side for the touchdown.

But a couple of plays earlier in that drive, Batch broke a metacarpal bone in his right hand.

— Game reports

To me, it looked like the game really slowed down for Charlie Batch. Last week, he was a little antsy, a little quick to try to do things. Today, the game slowed down. He made good decisions, he looked comfortable, he made good throws. He played himself back into game speed, and I think he played very solidly.

His hand is injured, his throwing hand. I think it's going to be a couple of weeks.

— Coach Bill Cowher

It was another game against an inferior opponent that had to be played, and won, with a roster missing several key components. It may not have been pretty, but the Steelers did what they needed to do.

It's been that way for three weeks now, and that's an attribute a team needs if it hopes to have its season extend to February.

— By Bob Labriola

Game 10

PITTSBURGH	13
BALTIMORE	16

Date: Nov. 20
Site: M&T Bank Stadium
Weather conditions:
56 degrees, sunny

Steelers leaders
Rushing: Willie Parker, 18 carries for 59 yards
Passing: Tommy Maddox, 19-for-36 for 230 yards, 1 TD, 1 INT
Receiving: Hines Ward, 6 catches for 81 yards
Defense: DE Aaron Smith, 7 tackles, 1 sack, 1 forced fumble

Key moment: A 25-yard pass from Maddox to Cedrick Wilson gave the Steelers a first down at their 48 on the first possession of overtime, but the drive ended when Maddox was sacked on third-and-4 from the Baltimore 46-yard line. The Steelers went three-and-out the other time they had the ball in overtime.

Steelers Digest Player of the Week: DE Aaron Smith

Quote to remember:
"It came down to the wire. We definitely felt like that was a team we weren't supposed to let hang around, because if you let them hang around, their confidence is going to build and that's what happened."
— LB Joey Porter

Cornerback Deshea Townsend stopped a Baltimore scoring threat when he picked off Kyle Boller in the first quarter.

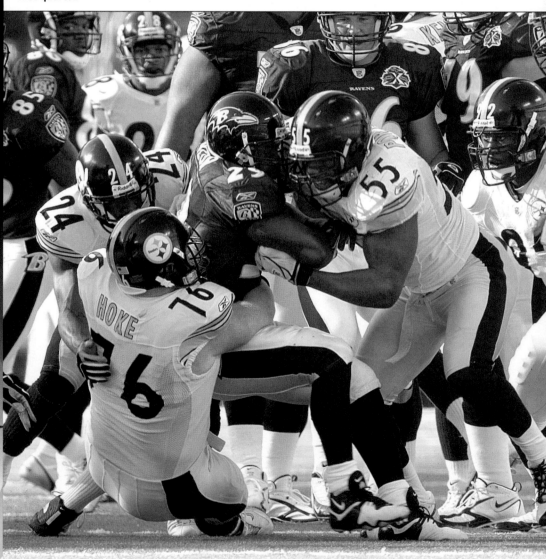

The Steelers defense shut down the Ravens running game, with Chris Hoke and Joey Porter taking care of Chester Taylor on this play.

Willie Parker didn't find that much running room against the Baltimore defense, finishing with 59 yards on 18 carries.

This had to be one massively uncomfortable moment for Baltimore running back Chester Taylor, who felt the full brunt of Casey Hampton's 300-plus pounds.

It's never a real good sign when the punter is a team's best player, but that was the case in the first half with the Steelers. On his four punts in the first half, Chris Gardocki averaged 51 yards.

Tommy Maddox attempted 36 passes, was sacked six times and forced to run three more times after a pass play broke down. That's 45 pass plays called with the No. 3 quarterback on the field in a game where the Steelers never trailed by more than one score.

— Game reports

Whenever a 7-2 goes against a 2-7 in the NFL, it's only news if the 7-2 loses, and that's exactly what happened here last Sunday. The 7-2 lost this game; arguing that it had chances to win but didn't is semantics.

The Steelers lost to the Ravens, 16-13, in overtime, and it was a team effort. Execution, strategy, poise, all of it. And they lost to the Ravens, a team that was just as injured, and also a team on the brink of giving up on its season.

— By Bob Labriola

We were not real efficient on the sideline. That's something that has not been indicative of us, but we were certainly not in rhythm on the sideline in terms of personnel groupings and getting plays in.

We had a lot more (penalties), some big ones. I don't know what Bryant McFadden was doing to get called twice on a punt, and we had more in the kicking game than we have had in the past. There were some inopportune flags at times, like the roughing the quarterback because we were off the field on third down.

— Coach Bill Cowher

Game 11

PITTSBURGH 7
INDIANAPOLIS 26

Date: Nov. 28
Site: RCA Dome
Outdoor weather:
57 degrees

Steelers leaders
Rushing: Willie Parker, 12 carries
for 43 yards
Passing: Ben Roethlisberger, 17-
for-26 for 133 yards, 1 TD, 2 INT
Receiving: Hines Ward,
3 catches for 28 yards, 1 TD
Defense: LB James Farrior,
9 tackles

Key moment: The Steelers
trailed 16-7 when Coach Bill
Cowher decided to try an onside
kick to start the second half. The
move backfired badly when the
Colts recovered at the Pittsburgh
37 and drove for a touchdown
that increased the lead to 16.

Steelers Digest
Player of the Week:
LB James Farrior

Quote to remember:
*"There's not much to say.
They pretty much dominated us.
Our offense to their defense, they
were pretty smothering out there,
and we really couldn't get
anything going. Their offense
and their defensive front pretty
much dominated tonight, and
you can't deny that."*
— Coach Bill Cowher

The Monday night battle at the RCA Dome hardly could have gotten off to a worse start for the Steelers, who watched Marvin Harrison score on an 80-yard pass play on Indianapolis' first offensive play.

The Steelers rebounded from their slow start and got themselves back in the game when Hines Ward's touchdown catch cut the Colts' lead to 10-7 late in the first quarter.

Now, it's a losing streak. It's a measurable deficit in the AFC North standings and not simply a function of having an earlier bye. It's also the reality of falling outside the conference's six spots reserved for those that qualify for the playoffs.

The Steelers lost to the Indianapolis Colts here last Monday night, but that alone is not their problem ... it's the cumulative effect of it all.

A loss to the Colts plus a loss to New England. Add in a giveaway to the Jaguars and a bad loss in Baltimore. That's four losses as December begins, which means there are only five more games left in the regular season.

The Steelers have taken their measure against the NFL's best, and their next fight is Sunday against the Cincinnati Bengals. That's the one they cannot afford to lose.

— By Bob Labriola

Based on the fact the Colts scored touchdowns on their first five possessions the previous week against the Bengals, it was important for the Steelers offense to string together some first downs to allow the defense to gather itself.

But in the battle along the line of scrimmage, the Colts defense got the better of the early play. On the Steelers' first two possessions, three runs netted minus-4 yards and Ben Roethlisberger was sacked once.

— Game reports

Troy Polamalu put Dwight Freeney's spin move to shame during his interception that set up the Steelers' touchdown. In keeping his angle on Marvin Harrison, the Steelers' strong safety rolled his hips without missing a step.

— By Jim Wexell

Linebacker Joey Porter caused a fumble when he sacked Peyton Manning in the second quarter, but the Steelers couldn't come up with the loose ball.

Safety Troy Polamalu set up the Steelers' only touchdown when he picked off Peyton Manning and returned the interception 36 yards to the Indianapolis 7-yard line.

Game 12

CINCINNATI	**38**
PITTSBURGH	**31**

Date: Dec. 4
Site: Heinz Field
Weather conditions:
30 degrees, cloudy

Steelers leaders
Rushing: Willie Parker, 15 carries
for 71 yards
Passing: Ben Roethlisberger, 29-
for-41 for 386 yards, 3 TD, 3 INT
Receiving: Hines Ward,
9 catches for 135 yards, 2 TD
Defense: CB Ike Taylor, 3 tackles,
2 passes defensed

Key moment: After trailing
38-24 in the fourth quarter, the
Steelers got the ball back with
2:26 left with a chance to tie.
But a holding penalty on the punt
return set the tone for an ugly
game-ending sequence that
included two penalties on the
offensive line and two sacks.

**Steelers Digest
Player of the Week:**
WR Hines Ward

Quote to remember:
*"We have to bounce back.
If anybody is questioning
themselves, they don't need
to be out here. I think this team
will bounce back strong,
hopefully stronger than ever.
We have to; there's no question."*
— **QB Ben Roethlisberger**

Cornerback Ricardo Colclough had good coverage on T.J. Houshmandzadeh on this first-quarter play, but still couldn't prevent the 43-yard touchdown pass.

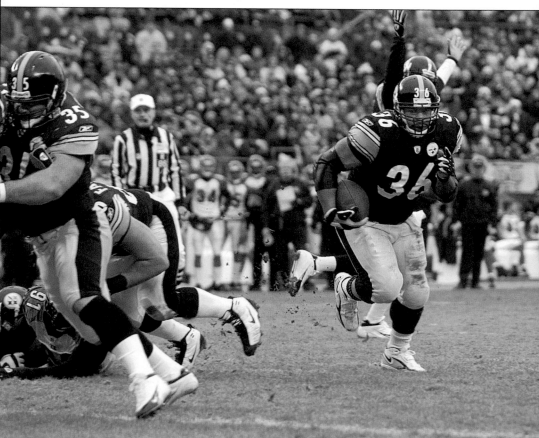

Jerome Bettis opened the scoring in what would become a shootout when he reached the end zone on a 1-yard run.

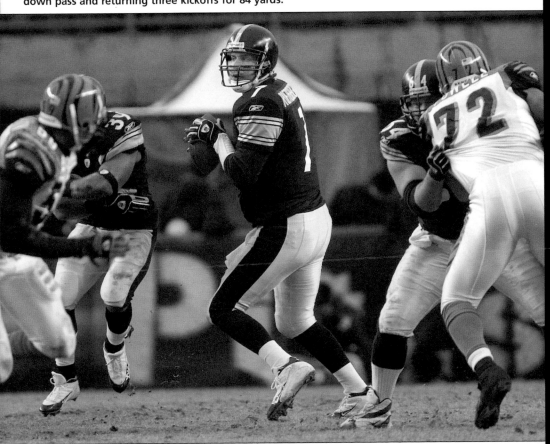

Quincy Morgan contributed in a couple of different ways against Cincinnati, catching a 25-yard touch-down pass and returning three kickoffs for 84 yards.

Ben Roethlisberger put up big passing numbers as the Steelers found themselves in the type of game that ran contrary to their preferred approach.

The Steelers were lured too quickly into a style that emphasized the Bengals' strengths. Against a defense that led the NFL with 33 takeaways, the Steelers put the ball in the air 41 times; they got into an up-and-down game with an offense that runs the field as well as any in the NFL outside of Indianapolis.

The Steelers are scrounging for scraps instead of vying for a seat at the main table because now they're 12 opponents into a schedule that contains 16, and they are facing life as a team that suddenly isn't showing the ability to be what it was built to be.

— By Bob Labriola

I will not question their effort. They fought until the very end. There were some obstacles that we created that we could not overcome.

Like I told the team, at this point just play it out. The important thing is that we come back and talk about where we are and play the hand that's dealt us. That's the most important thing that you can do.

— Coach Bill Cowher

The Bengals used special teams to create huge advantages in field position at a time when they needed it most — following two Steelers touchdowns. After the Steelers scored for a 14-7 lead in the first quarter, Tab Perry returned the kickoff 46 yards to jump-start a 53-yard touchdown drive; after the Steelers tied it at 24-24 in the third quarter, Perry returned the kickoff 94 yards to the 3-yard line.

— Game reports

The Steelers will finish with a four-game winning streak and make the playoffs. I've bet a sandwich and a beer on it. If I win, the offensive linemen are invited to share because they would be the reason.

— By Jim Wexell

Game 13

| CHICAGO | 9 |
| PITTSBURGH | 21 |

Date: Dec. 11
Site: Heinz Field
Weather conditions:
32 degrees, cloudy
with snow flurries

Steelers leaders
Rushing: Jerome Bettis,
17 carries for 101 yards, 2 TD
Passing: Ben Roethlisberger, 13-
for-20 for 173 yards, 1 TD, 0 INT
Receiving: Hines Ward,
3 catches for 27 yards, 1 TD
Defense: LB James Farrior,
11 tackles, 1 pass defensed

Key moment: After the
Steelers took a 7-0 lead on the
opening possession, Chicago
answered with a drive that led to
a first-and-goal from the 2-yard
line. But Clark Haggans' sack on
second down forced the Bears to
settle for a field goal.

**Steelers Digest
Player of the Week:**
RB Jerome Bettis

Quote to remember:
*"This game set up for me in terms
of the conditions and the field.
I get a head of steam going, and
they have to play off blocks, and
it's hard for those guys to stay in
there and get leverage on me.
So this type of weather is very
beneficial to me."*
— **RB Jerome Bettis**

After rushing for 100 yards in the second half alone, Jerome Bettis said the driving snow at Heinz Field was perfectly suited to his style.

By the second
half, it became
very difficult
to see across
the field.

Hines Ward's 14-yard touchdown reception gave the Steelers a 7-0 lead less than six minutes into the game, and they never looked back.

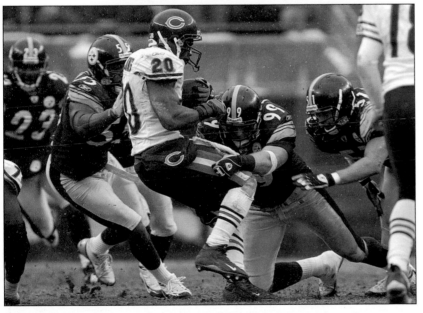

The defense never gave Thomas Jones and the rest of the Chicago offense much of a chance.

From the Pages of
Steelers Digest

We talked a lot about confidence (on the night before the game). State of mind, being certain and having trust, that's the definition of confidence. State of mind is a choice. These guys had to make a choice.

— Coach Bill Cowher

As he has so many times for this team, Jerome Bettis provided exactly what the Steelers needed at the precise time they needed it. In the first half, Bettis had one carry for 1 yard (a touchdown), but in the second half, with the Steelers protecting a lead, he carried 16 times for 100 yards, and he finished with two touchdowns.

◆◆◆

The team's first offensive play was a run that lost 1 yard, but on the next, a screen pass to Willie Parker, Alan Faneca (on DT Ian Scott) and Jeff Hartings (on MLB Brian Urlacher) made the blocks that created a 45-yard gain. That got the Steelers off to a good start. Criticized, and rightly so, for the performances during the three-game losing streak, the offensive line deserves a lot of praise for the work it did against one of the best defensive lines in football.

— Game reports

The key play of the game plan was executed into the key play of the game. The Steelers hoped to slow the aggressive and speedy Bears defenders right off the bat, so they wanted to hit them early with Fast Willie Parker.

"We knew going into the game our second play was going to be the screen pass," said Parker. "So we took a lot of their aggressiveness away early. They were just sitting back after that thinking, 'What are they going to do to us next? What are they going to do to us next?' We just played our type of game today."

— By Jim Wexell

Game 14

PITTSBURGH   18
MINNESOTA   3

Date: Dec. 18
Site: Metrodome
Outdoor weather: 3 degrees

Steelers leaders
Rushing: Willie Parker, 14 carries for 81 yards
Passing: Ben Roethlisberger, 10-for-15 for 149 yards, 0 TD, 0 INT
Receiving: Heath Miller, 2 catches for 58 yards
Defense: LB Larry Foote, 7 tackles, 1 sack, 1 safety

Key moment: The Steelers led 3-0 in the first quarter when Minnesota recovered an Antwaan Randle El muff on a punt return at the Pittsburgh 3-yard line. But after the Steelers stuffed Ciatrick Fason for a 1-yard loss on third-and-goal from the 1, Minnesota settled for a field goal. The Steelers thwarted another first-and-goal situation in the second quarter when linebacker Joey Porter intercepted Brad Johnson on second down.

Steelers Digest Player of the Week:
LB Larry Foote

Quote to remember:
"Our focus was great all week. I don't think that had anything to do with it. They just beat our butts."
— **Vikings QB Brad Johnson**

Joey Porter stopped a Minnesota scoring threat when he intercepted Brad Johnson on second-and-goal early in the second quarter.

Steelers players were only too glad to help referee Ed Hochuli call a safety after Larry Foote and Joey Porter combined to tackle running back Michael Bennett in the end zone.

Kimo von Oelhoffen preserved the Steelers' 10-3 lead in the third quarter when he blocked this 32-yard field goal attempt by Paul Edinger.

Antwaan Randle El highlighted a huge day for the special teams with this 72-yard punt return, which set up the only touchdown of the game.

If it was more than just lip service, if they truly had righted themselves, they come here and win. If they really had learned anything from the Wednesdays in full pads, they come here and win. If they were going to get into the playoffs and then do something when they got there, they come here and expose this Vikings team as the cupcake-eating champion it is.

There comes a time during every NFL season when a team has to separate itself from the mediocre and prove it deserves to advance to the postseason to compete for the sport's ultimate prize.

This was that time for the Steelers, and they did not fail.

— By Bob Labriola

The Vikings are No. 1 in the NFC and No. 4 in the National Football League (in kickoff returns). We didn't want to give up big plays. Our coverage teams did a good job. Jeff Reed did a good job kicking it. He squibbed it one time, he pooched it one time, just tried to disrupt their timing because they are a pretty special kickoff return group.

Our punt coverage did a great job. The return by Antwaan Randle El was a big turning point in the game, the punt return that we had in the first half. Those guys came up big today.

— Coach Bill Cowher

Sometimes statistics can reflect dominance. In the first half, the Vikings had six offensive possessions. They ended: punt, punt, field goal on a drive that netted just 1 yard; interception; three-and-out; interception.

◆◆◆

In the 27 regular season games played in December and January since 2000, the Steelers are 21-6 (.778). They are 2-1 in December this season.

— Game reports

Game 15

PITTSBURGH 41
CLEVELAND 0

Date: Dec. 24
Site: Cleveland Browns Stadium

Weather conditions:
44 degrees, sunny

Steelers leaders
Rushing: Willie Parker, 17 carries for 130 yards, 1 TD
Passing: Ben Roethlisberger, 13-for-20 for 226 yards, 1 TD, 0 INT
Receiving: Hines Ward, 7 catches for 105 yards, 1 TD
Defense: LB Joey Porter, 5 tackles, 3 sacks, 1 forced fumble

Key moment: This was domination from start to finish. The Steelers held Cleveland without a first down on the first possession of the game, then converted three third downs to take a 7-0 lead, the last coming when Jerome Bettis ran 2 yards for the touchdown on third-and-goal.

Steelers Digest Player of the Week:
LB Joey Porter

Quote to remember:
"This was one of those games where we clicked really well on offense. Our defense was out there having fun flying around. It was fun watching them today. We had a good day, and it felt good for us."

— QB Ben Roethlisberger

Cleveland rookie quarterback Charlie Frye never had a chance in the face of a relentless pass rush that produced eight sacks, including three by Joey Porter (55).

The Steelers' first two drives ended in touchdowns, the second coming on Hines Ward's 7-yard reception.

Willie Parker approaches the end zone toward the end of his 80-yard touchdown run, which made the score 27-0 in the third quarter.

James Harrison (92) partially blocked this second-quarter Cleveland punt, which wound up traveling only 8 yards and gave the Steelers the ball at midfield.

I like to think we are getting better as a football team, and we need to do that. We are starting to get people back. Our quarterback is starting to look like he's in rhythm ...

... We got the offense going. Our special teams were outstanding today. Our coverage teams were good. We got the big return by Antwaan Randle El. We block a punt. We haven't had kick blocks in back-to-back games since I've been here. We are starting to do some things well, and we need to at this time of year.

— Coach Bill Cowher

The Steelers hit everything that moved, from Jerome Bettis barreling into Ben Taylor for the first touchdown to Larry Foote drilling Aaron Shea short of the goal line on the last play. It was a stunning display from beginning to end.

As you probably have figured out by now, the Steelers thrive when they're forgotten, disrespected, kicked to the curb. So if you want them to roll through the soft defenses in Cincinnati and Indianapolis, don't tell them how good they are.

— By Jim Wexell

During their three-game losing streak, the Steelers turned the ball over eight times; in their three wins since then they've turned it over twice. The offensive line has handled three opponents in a row, and it dominated the last two. Penalties are down, third-down conversions are up. And their defense has cut down on the points allowed from nine to three to zip.

"We made a statement," said James Harrison. "Margin of victory, stuff like that, is nice, but winning and going to the playoffs is our goal."

The playoffs are coming. So are the Steelers.

— By Bob Labriola

Game 16

DETROIT	**21**
PITTSBURGH	**35**

Date: Jan. 1
Site: Heinz Field
Weather conditions:
39 degrees, cloudy

Steelers leaders
Rushing: Willie Parker, 26 carries
for 135 yards
Passing: Ben Roethlisberger, 7-
for-16 for 135 yards, 0 TD, 2 INT
Receiving: Heath Miller,
3 catches for 62 yards
Defense: LB James Farrior,
9 tackles, 1 sack, 1 forced fumble

Key moment: After the
Steelers scored a touchdown on
the first drive of the second half
to go up 28-14, Detroit answered
with a touchdown to make it a
seven-point game again. But the
Steelers responded with an
82-yard touchdown drive highlighted by a 43-yard completion
from Roethlisberger to Miller.

**Steelers Digest
Player of the Week:**
FB Dan Kreider

Quote to remember:
*"Let me just say this, I can't say
enough about our special teams.
To me that was the only thing that
was on today. We didn't play
well enough offensively and
defensively, but I can't say
enough about our special teams."*

— Coach Bill Cowher

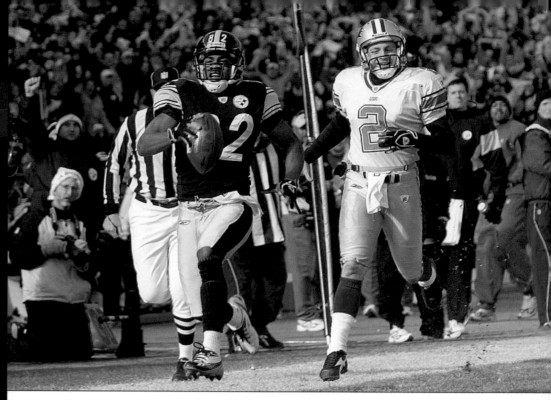

Antwaan Randle El got the new year started on the right foot with an 81-yard punt return that gave the Steelers a quick 7-0 lead.

In addition to Randle El's touchdown, the special teams also created a turnover when Chidi Iwuoma forced this Eddie Drummond fumble and Brett Keisel recovered the loose ball.

The Steelers completed only seven passes against Detroit, but two of them were good for 40 yards or more, including tight end Heath Miller's 43-yard gain in the third quarter.

Troy Polamalu stopped a Detroit drive in the second quarter when he knocked the ball loose from fullback Paul Smith and defensive end Aaron Smith recovered the fumble.

From the Pages of
Steelers Digest

I have so much appreciation for Jerome, and he's always been there. He's going to be one of those guys who when the day comes and he's not there, there's going to be a void because it seems like he's always been there every week.

We've been through a lot together, and I have a tremendous appreciation — more than I can even express — for what he stands for as a football player, but more so for what he stands for as a person. For every yard he's gained on the field, this guy, in my mind, has exceeded that off the field — the kind of individual he is, the way he gives back and what he stands for. I've not been around many guys like him.

— Coach Bill Cowher

They don't have a 15-1 record. Or home-field advantage. Or any recognition as the best team in the AFC.

But as the NFL playoffs begin, these Pittsburgh Steelers are a better team, they are more capable of handling what the NFL playoffs are all about. And they are better and more capable, because Ben Roethlisberger is better and more capable ...

... Said Bettis, "I think right now, Ben is the face of this team."

As the 2005 playoffs begin, Ben Roethlisberger is more than just the face of the Steelers. He's also their best hope for them.

— By Bob Labriola

Deep down, the Steelers have to be elated with their (playoff) draw.

"I am," said Brett Keisel. "We know we can go into Cincinnati and win. We've done it before, and I think we have a little chip on our shoulder. They came in here and stole one from us."

And now the Steelers want it back.

— By Jim Wexell

BEN,
THANKS FOR
THE DANCE,
BUT I'M STILL
A BROWNS FAN!
KRISTY♥
PS- CALL ME!

BIG
BEN
←ME
←ME

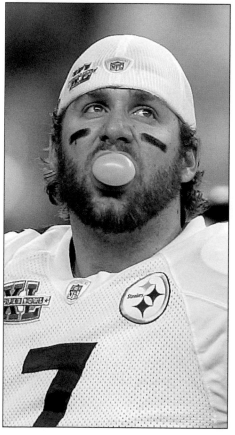

Playoffs

Big Ben comes up huge

They didn't care. They really didn't. When a team had to win four straight and also get some help just to make the playoffs, there isn't a lot of extra energy to expend on making a list of preferred opponents.

The Steelers officially had been in the playoffs for about 15 minutes thanks to their season-ending win over the Detroit Lions, but the New England Patriots and Miami Dolphins still were waltzing around the floor of Gillette Stadium in the game that would set the matchups for AFC Wild Card Weekend; the dates and kickoff times were a foregone conclusion.

Because of the size of the Boston television market, ABC wanted the Patriots for its 8:30 p.m. slot on Saturday, and that meant the other AFC contest would be played in Cincinnati on Sunday at 4:30 p.m. because CBS was getting the bone of having an NFL playoff game lead into its prime-time programming. If New England defeated Miami in the regular season finale, the Steelers would be their opponent. If the Dolphins won, Jacksonville was headed to Foxboro and the Steelers would be sent to Cincinnati for a rubber match with the Bengals.

As Coach Bill Cowher sat down at the table to begin his news conference after the Lions game, televisions above his head were tuned to the action in New England. That game was coming down to a two-point conversion attempt, and Cowher noticed a portion of the media was distracted.

"You guys watching something?" asked Cowher. When updated on the situation, Cowher asked if they all wanted to wait and watch the deciding play. A reporter answered that with his own question: "Don't you?" Cowher just shrugged and answered, "Nah. Let me know." But once that two-point conversion pass failed and it

officially was the Bengals in Round 1, the chance to avenge themselves became a primary motivating force for the Steelers.

In the late afternoon of Dec. 4, the Bengals had turned Heinz Field into their personal playground in the final stages of the 38-31 win remembered by Steelers fans mostly as being the third of the three-game losing streak that was killing their pre-Christmas spirit. T.J. Houshmandzadeh made a show for the cameras of wiping off his cleats with a Terrible Towel in the tunnel leading to the locker room; Chad Johnson talked enough to pull a vocal cord, and did it all while wearing a Terrible Towel as a bib; and the whole thing reeked of a victory parade even though all the win did was put Cincinnati in control of the AFC North Division race. "It's always good to beat the Steelers," said Bengals defensive lineman John Thornton, with a big smile and a wink.

Still in the Steelers' locker room getting dressed, Jerome Bettis had been told of some of the things coming from the Bengals locker room just across the way. Bettis suppressed the urge to fire back and then said, "You know what? They can talk all they want. They won. We have to take it." The 2005 NFL playoffs were going to give the Steelers an opportunity for some payback, and those close to the team knew well that nothing motivates this particular group of players more.

The Bengals knew enough about the Steelers to understand how physical a playoff game against them would be, and they were ready and held their own in that aspect in the early stages, but where their postseason inexperience manifested itself was a lack of poise. When Carson Palmer was lost to a knee injury on a hit from Kimo von Oelhoffen that neither was flagged nor deserved to be, the Bengals lost their composure. Instead of re-

focusing their own players — because the injury happened on the Bengals' second offensive play of the game — the Cincinnati coaches were screaming at Steelers players from the sideline. Their reaction sent the message that the game had been stolen from them because of Palmer's injury, and at the time the score was 0-0 with more than 10 minutes to play in the first quarter. Then when things got tough, as inevitably happens in the NFL playoffs, the players could take the cue and their excuse was ready-made.

Cincinnati would build a couple of 10-point leads in the first half, but on each occasion Ben Roethlisberger and the offense answered with a touchdown drive to tighten things back up. The second of those responses came late in the first half when Roethlisberger was 3-for-3 for 74 of the drive's 76 yards, plus the touchdown to Hines Ward. It was a microcosm of a stunning performance by Roethlisberger, who had been a liability in the 2004

Quarterback Ben Roethlisberger trots off the field after the Steelers stun the top-seeded Indianapolis Colts at the RCA Dome.

playoffs but who opened his second go-around in the postseason by completing 14 of 19 for 208 yards with three touchdowns and no interceptions in a 31-17 win.

One of the benefits of being the sixth seed in the AFC was the Steelers knew that if they advanced to the Divisional Playoff round their opponent had to be No. 1 seed Indianapolis. This was another opportunity for some payback, because the Colts had handled the Steelers on a Monday night in late November, but any disappointment in the outcome was mitigated by what they had learned from the experience. From the very start of Cowher's tenure as coach, the Steelers would prepare for particularly difficult venues by setting up speakers during practice to simulate the problems they were going to encounter because of crowd noise, but nothing they could manufacture was comparable to what they actually experienced on Nov. 28 in the RCA Dome.

The way the Steelers defense had played in the 26-7 loss gave the team hope that if they could get some of the problems they had offensively squared away, there was going to be a real chance for them to pull off the upset. It all would start with them mastering their own version of a silent count, a procedure where everyone would key off a signal from center Jeff Hartings to determine when the ball would

be snapped. The silent count would give the offensive linemen a better chance against the aggressive, turf-aided Colts defensive front, but parlor tricks were only going to get them so far. If they were going to win this game, they were going to have to force the Colts to play 60 minutes of Steelers football, and that wouldn't happen if they fell behind early.

Because of the magnitude of this game, the press box was stocked with the same national media types who long ago had traded a portion of their professional objectivity to become card-carrying members of the Peyton Manning fan club, but before the first half of this AFC Divisional Playoff game was over it was clear the best quarterback on the field was the guy wearing the white No. 7 jersey. On the game's opening possession, Roethlisberger completed 6 of 7 for 76 yards and a touchdown; the only incompletion was a drop, and his first two strikes against Tony Dungy's famed cover-2 were to Heath Miller over the middle, at the defense's soft underbelly.

The Colts went three-and-out on each of their opening two possessions before Roethlisberger struck again. On a third-and-10 from the Pittsburgh 39-yard line, he found Ward for 45; two plays later, it was another strike to Miller over the middle, and it was 14-0 with 3:12 still to play in the first quarter. All of a sudden, the Colts were in the type of game they were ill-equipped to play, and all of their warts were revealed under the glare of this national spotlight. One first-half Indianapolis possession lasted 15 plays and consumed more than nine minutes and yielded only three points, while a Steelers possession in the fourth quarter ended in a punt but not before it sucked eight minutes off the clock.

The Steelers had established their physical dominance to this point in the game and held a 21-10 lead when referee Peter Morelli overturned a Troy Polamalu interception in the kind of ruling that could have sent a lesser team into a death spiral. If the play was ruled correctly, the Steelers probably chewed up the remaining 5:26 after Polamalu's interception with their running game, and maybe score again. Had that happened, Manning would have finished 16-of-29 for 205 yards, with no touchdowns and one interception. As it was, the Steelers needed to dip into the well of their resolve and make the kinds of big plays in critical situations that served to show the rest of the NFL they had the stuff of champions throughout the final stages of this 21-18 win.

On two straight possessions after the Colts had closed to

Cornerback Ike Taylor's interception late in the second quarter helped the Steelers build a 24-3 halftime lead in the AFC Championship Game at Denver.

within three points, the Steelers defense stoned a guy who already has received some media support as the greatest quarterback in NFL history. On the first of those, Manning was 1-for-2 for 2 yards with two sacks that turned the ball over on downs on the Colts 2-yard line; on the second, he was 2-for-4 for 30 yards but back-to-back incompletions had Mike Vanderjagt attempting the tying field goal from 46 yards away. And one final volley on the subject of this game's two quarterbacks: Think Peyton Manning is a good enough athlete to make that tackle in the open field after Jerome Bettis' fumble was picked up by Nick Harper on a dead run? Me neither.

This set up an AFC Championship Game pitting a Denver Broncos team that was undefeated at home in 2005, a team with a home-field advantage made more daunting by the mile-high altitude, versus a Steelers team on a run that could make it the best road team in NFL playoff history. It was no contest. Due respect to the Broncos, who had finished 13-3 to earn the AFC's No. 2 seed and the bye that came with it, who had taken out the two-time defending champion New England Patriots to host this conference championship, but this game was over at halftime.

Again, it was Roethlisberger who led them. Apparently not convinced what they had seen him do to the Colts was real, the Broncos figured the Steelers to start by trying to run the ball and they aligned their defense accordingly. Bad move. In fashioning a 10-0 lead, Roethlisberger was 7-for-8 for 89 yards and the touchdown, and on the Steelers' other two touchdown drives of the half he completed 6 of 9 for 91 yards and another score.

But it wasn't just the Steelers offense that dominated. In helping build that 24-3 halftime lead, the defense had limited the Broncos' No. 5-ranked offense to six first downs and 38 yards rushing while forcing two turnovers; Jeff Reed's 47-yard field goal 10 minutes into the game had established a positive dynamic right off the bat for the Steelers, and the combination of his kickoffs and coverage had made Denver's average drive start its own 28-yard line. In fact, after the game's first 30 minutes, the only statistical categories in which the Broncos had posted higher numbers were turnovers and punts.

Still, these playoff games are the times when teams truly need great quarterback play, and the Steelers got it from Roethlisberger. In the win over the Bengals, and in the first halves against Indianapolis and Denver, Roethlisberger completed 39 of 55 for 560 yards, with seven touchdowns and one interception for a passer rating of 135.6. It was a string of remarkable performances by a quarterback who outplayed the guy on the other team, head-to-head, in three straight road playoff wins, but also a guy who finished seventh in the AFC balloting for the Pro Bowl. Yes, seventh.

The Steelers were going to the Super Bowl, and the story of Jerome Bettis capping a magnificent career with a return to his hometown for a shot to go out as a champion would dominate the worldwide sporting press for the next fortnight. But the Steelers winning this AFC Championship Game also meant Ben Roethlisberger had kept two promises he made, promises that at the time sounded mostly like youthful bravado. On Jan. 23, he went up to Bettis on the sideline at Heinz Field as the Patriots were wrapping up the 2004 AFC championship and promised through tears that if retirement could be postponed for another year he'd get him to that Super Bowl. And on Aug. 1, he told reporters who were asking about the possibility of a sophomore slump, "All you guys think I'm going to have it, so I'm not going to. We can still win a Super Bowl and not win 15 (regular season) games."

On to Detroit.

WILD CARD
PLAYOFFS
NFL

| PITTSBURGH | 31 |
| CINCINNATI | 17 |

Date: Jan. 8

Site: Paul Brown Stadium

Weather conditions:
61 degrees, partly cloudy

Steelers leaders
Rushing:
Jerome Bettis,
10 carries for 52 yards, 1 TD
Passing:
Ben Roethlisberger,
14-for-19 for 208 yards,
3 TD, 0 INT
Receiving:
Cedrick Wilson,
3 catches for 104 yards, 1 TD
Defense:
LB James Farrior,
4 tackles, 1 interception

The Steelers get ready to begin their playoff journey at Cincinnati's Paul Brown Stadium.

The game took a dramatic turn on Cincinnati's first possession when quarterback Carson Palmer sustained a torn ACL after being hit by defensive end Kimo von Oelhoffen.

Touchdowns by Hines Ward (top) in the second quarter and Jerome Bettis (bottom) in the third quarter helped the Steelers turn a 17-7 deficit into a 21-17 lead they would continue to build on.

Although the play appeared to go off without a hitch, Ben Roethlisberger wasn't certain "Fake 38 Direct Throwback" would work until Cedrick Wilson settled under a 43-yard pass and ambled into the end zone at Paul Brown Stadium.

"I faked like (the snap) was over my head," said Roethlisberger in explaining the play that broke the Bengals' backs. "I saw the cornerback come toward me, and I'm like, 'Oh boy, he's going to stay here and watch me.' I kind of played possum, and he ran after Antwaan (Randle El). I'm sitting there waiting for Antwaan to throw me the ball. He went about 10 yards farther than he was supposed to.

"The ball hung up there forever. When I was catching it, I just knew it was going to be man coverage. I caught it, and it was man coverage."

— By Mike Prisuta

Answering scores with scores kept the Steelers in the game at halftime even though the defense allowed the Bengals to score on three of their four possessions. But each of the Steelers' first-half touchdown drives followed touchdowns by the Bengals. On those two possessions, Roethlisberger completed 5 of 7 for 98 yards and both touchdowns.

In two games in Cincinnati, he completed 23 of 38 for 290 yards with four touchdowns and two interceptions.

◆◆◆

After a slow start, the Steelers offense scored four touchdowns over five possessions in the middle two quarters to take command of the game, and then the defense recorded takeaways on two of the Bengals' final three possessions to clinch it.

— Game reports

PITTSBURGH	31
CINCINNATI	17

Key moment:

The Steelers had taken a 21-17 lead earlier in the third quarter when they faced a third-and-3 from the Cincinnati 43-yard line. That's when they pulled out a gadget play that worked to perfection, with Roethlisberger handing off to Antwaan Randle El, who threw back to Roethlisberger, who then hit Wilson with a 43-yard TD pass.

Steelers Digest Player of the Week:
QB Ben Roethlisberger

Quote to remember:

"Everyone said that if we couldn't run the ball, we couldn't win. The offensive line did a great job of opening things up for me, giving me time, picking up the blitzes, and so our passing game really stepped up today."

— QB Ben Roethlisberger

Troy Polamalu ended Cincinnati's last drive with an interception. He then lateralled to Chris Hope, whose nice return (bottom) was negated by a penalty.

Cedrick Wilson was on the receiving end of a perfectly executed trick play that produced a huge 43-yard touchdown that gave the Steelers a 28-17 lead late in the third quarter.

Linebacker Joey Porter led the victory celebration in the charged-up Steelers locker room.

"It's time for a change. It's like going from a black-and-white TV to a color TV. It was Pittsburgh; now it's Cincinnati, and it'll probably be that way for a while now.

— Chad Johnson, after the Bengals' 38-31 win at Heinz Field

"This is what it's all about — the loser goes home. We put Pittsburgh back on the map of the AFC North. They may have won the (division) championship, but we are still alive in the playoffs.

"For them to make a rap video, that was disrespectful to us."

— Hines Ward

"Guys were jawing. I was having personal battles with their coaching staff. They made it seem as if that play (when Kimo von Oelhoffen's hit injured Carson Palmer's knee) was intentional. That was a clean play between the whistles.

"They were just so mad. They felt that once Palmer got hurt, they were done. We had four or five guys go down ... we didn't sit up there and cry and harp about it. It happened. It's football."

— Joey Porter

Those are the emotions in this game. There was a lot being said leading up to the game, none of which I want to get into. We understand that. This is a rivalry game. This is a rivalry team, and the playoffs are here. There was a lot building up to this game.

There was a lot of emotion, and what happened to Carson, there was nothing that was done intentionally. I would think no one would even interpret it that way.

— Coach Bill Cowher

"Who dey?"

"We dey!"

— Chant in Steelers locker room

DIVISIONAL PLAYOFFS
NFL

PITTSBURGH	21
INDIANAPOLIS	18

Date: Jan. 15

Site: RCA Dome

Outdoor weather:
32 degrees

Steelers leaders
Rushing:
Willie Parker,
17 carries for 59 yards
Passing:
Ben Roethlisberger,
14-for-24 for 197 yards,
2 TD, 1 INT
Receiving:
Heath Miller,
3 catches for 61 yards, 1 TD
Defense:
LB James Farrior,
10 tackles, 2.5 sacks

Antwaan Randle El capped an impressive first drive for the Steelers with a 6-yard touchdown catch on third-and-3.

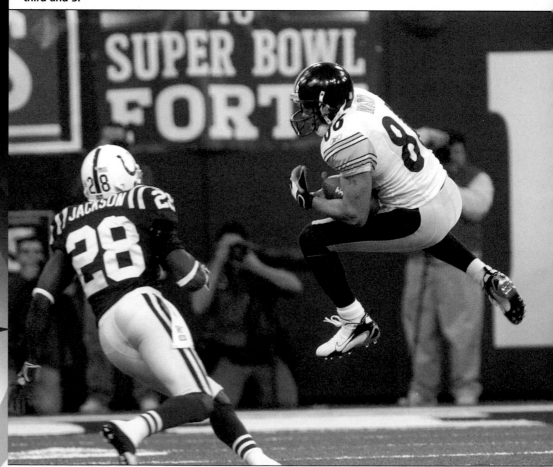

The Steelers came out firing on offense against the Colts, and Hines Ward already had three receptions after the first play of the second quarter.

Guard Kendall Simmons found himself helmet-less and on his back in the end zone as Jerome Bettis crossed the goal line to give the Steelers a 21-3 lead in the third quarter.

Any recipe for a Steelers win over the Colts included a solid start by the offense, but what the unit did in the first quarter exceeded all reasonable expectations. On the team's two touchdown drives, which covered 84 and 72 yards, Ben Roethlisberger was 8-for-10 for 128 yards, with two touchdowns and no interceptions.

Coach Bill Cowher preached about the importance of not taking any foolish penalties, and apparently his words were heeded. The Steelers were penalized twice for 8 yards. One was an intentional delay of game penalty taken to give punter Chris Gardocki a bit more room, and the other was a defensive offside on third-and-goal from the 6-yard line. But even after that penalty, the Colts had to settle for a field goal.

The Colts got the ball with 2:31 remaining, and they had all three of their timeouts remaining in a game they trailed 21-18. Starting at the Colts 18-yard line, the Steelers defense turned in three straight big plays.

A short pass from Peyton Manning to Edgerrin James gained 2 yards; Joey Porter sacked Manning for a loss of 8 to set up a third-and-16 at the 12-yard line; and after an incomplete pass, Porter and James Farrior shared a sack of Manning that turned the ball over on downs at the Colts 2-yard line.

In taking a 14-0 lead in the first quarter, offensive coordinator Ken Whisenhunt called eight running plays and 13 passes. On a six-play, 30-yard touchdown drive in the third quarter that gave them a 21-3 lead, he called all runs. In the second half, he called 29 runs and five passes.
    — Game reports

Ben Roethlisberger attempted only five passes in the second half as the Steelers went to work on the clock playing with the lead.

DIVISIONAL PLAYOFFS
NFL

| PITTSBURGH | 21 |
| INDIANAPOLIS | 18 |

Key moment: Even after Roethlisberger stopped Indy's Nick Harper after Jerome Bettis' fumble at the 1-yard line, there still was work to do. The Colts quickly drove to the Steelers 28-yard line, and on second down Bryant McFadden's tight coverage broke up Peyton Manning's pass to Reggie Wayne in the end zone. Two plays later, Mike Vanderjagt missed a 46-yard field goal attempt.

**Steelers Digest
Player of the Week:**
LB James Farrior

Quote to remember:
"You can't put it on any individual group. We played great as a team today. I think we played pretty good the first time we played this team. It's just that today we put together a team effort, and that's why we won this game."

— S Troy Polamalu

James Farrior (51) and Joey Porter (55) led a relentless pass rush that produced five sacks against Peyton Manning, including two on a key fourth-quarter possession.

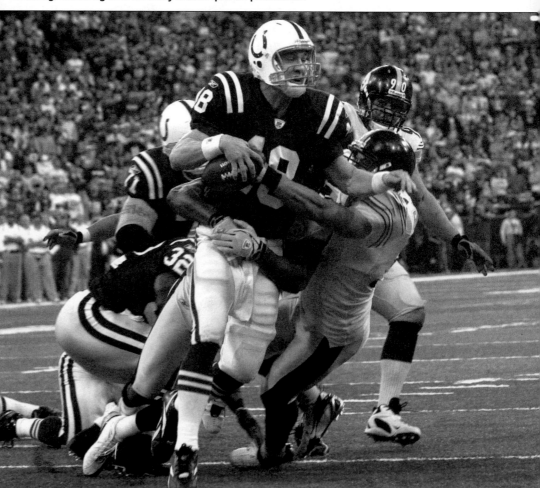

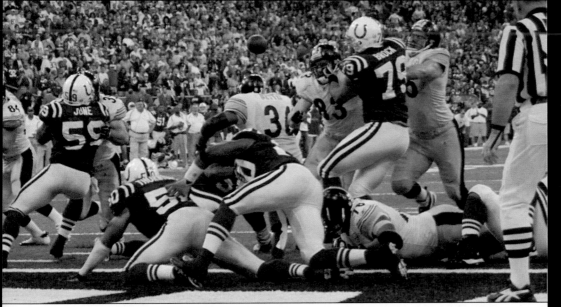

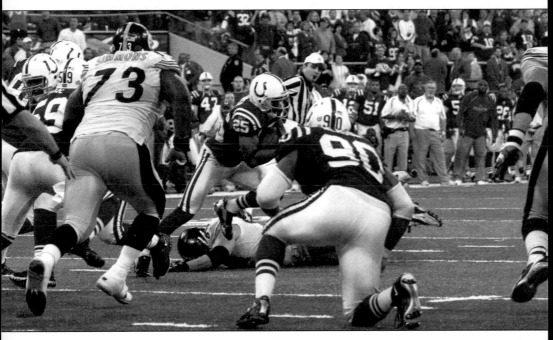

Jerome Bettis was on his way to slamming the door on the Colts when his fumble near the goal line set in motion one of the strangest plays in NFL playoff history. Fortunately for the Steelers, Ben Roethlisberger was able to tackle Nick Harper to prevent what could have been a 93-yard touchdown.

"My first reaction is to go get the ball, but I knew I wasn't going to get there in time. So then it's, 'Let's try to slow him down, do something so our guys can come up and make a play.' I think I turned him around enough times that he got close to me, and then he couldn't decide which way to go. So then I just saw his leg, and I went and I grabbed it. Luckily, he went down."

— **Ben Roethlisberger**

"It went from an all-time high, to an all-time low ... back to an all-time high."

— **Hines Ward**

It was going to take a superior effort, starting with the week's first team meeting, through every practice, until the game clock told them to stop. It was going to take every player performing at a career-best level, with each guy also walking the line of physical/aggressive vs. taking penalties/losing poise. It was going to take a flawless marriage of strategy and execution.

They got it. They got it all.

The Pittsburgh Steelers have been in the business of winning football games for 73 years, and what they did here last Sunday deserves to be recognized as among their best. There may not have been a trophy presentation at the end of it, but the Steelers took out the guys who were supposed to win it, and they did it in their dome ...

... On Jan. 24, 2005, the Steelers bemoaned the opportunity they had squandered the previous day in losing the AFC Championship Game to the New England Patriots, and they talked about the hard work that would be required to get back to that point again.

They're back.

— **By Bob Labriola**

A CHAMPIONSHIP GAME
NFL

PITTSBURGH   **34**
DENVER   **17**

Date: Jan. 22

Site: Invesco Field at Mile High

Weather conditions:
34 degrees, sunny

Steelers leaders
Rushing:
Jerome Bettis,
15 carries for 39 yards, 1 TD
Passing:
Ben Roethlisberger,
21-for-29 for 275 yards,
2 TD, 0 INT
Receiving:
Cedrick Wilson,
5 catches for 92 yards, 1 TD
Defense:
DE Brett Keisel,
4 tackles, 2 sacks,
1 forced fumble

Ben Roethlisberger listens to some tunes as he arrives at the Steelers team hotel in Denver.

The Steelers gather for a pregame prayer before taking the field for the AFC Championship Game.

Ben Roethlisberger was almost flawless in the first half, completing 13 of 17 passes for 180 yards with two touchdowns and no interceptions.

Jerome Bettis' 3-yard touchdown run immediately after the two-minute warning gave the Steelers a 17-3 lead, but they weren't done with their first-half scoring yet.

From the Pages of
Steelers Digest

To be able to come in here and do this is a tribute to the players who were out there on that field. We have a resilient group, with a young quarterback who didn't play young today. I can't say enough about this football team. We kind of traveled the hard road, and I think in the course of it, we probably grew as a football team and grew individually. Now we have an opportunity and hopefully we can finish the season off with one more win. That will be our intention.

Nothing drives me more than to hopefully be able to hand Mr. Rooney the fifth trophy. Nothing would make me more satisfied than to be able to do that.

— **Coach Bill Cowher**

Joey Porter didn't want to talk about how well he's been playing during the Steelers' march to Super Bowl XL.

"It doesn't matter how well I played," said Porter, "it's about how well our team is playing. I'm going to do what I have to do to win football games.

"It doesn't matter what I did. We're going to Detroit, and that's all that matters."

The Steelers are headed to Detroit and Super Bowl XL thanks in no small part to the relentless efforts of Porter and a defense that refused to give Broncos quarterback Jake Plummer room to breathe ...

... "Pressure is always the key with any quarterback," said Porter. "I never met a quarterback who likes pressure. I never met a quarterback who likes to be hit."

— **By Mike Prisuta**

"When you put people's backs to the wall, they can either crumble or they can start fighting back. We showed the Samurai spirit. We just have to continue to show that."

— **Troy Polamalu**

CHAMPIONSHIP GAME
NFL

| PITTSBURGH | 34 |
| DENVER | 17 |

Key moment: Bettis' touchdown run extended the Steelers' lead to 17-3 on the first play after the two-minute warning, but they weren't done in the first half just yet. On the first play of Denver's drive, Ike Taylor intercepted Jake Plummer, setting up Roethlisberger's TD pass to Hines Ward with seven seconds left. Just like that, the score went from 10-3 to 24-3.

Steelers Digest Player of the Week:
QB Ben Roethlisberger

Quote to remember:
"We knew we had a lot of hard work ahead of us after Week 12, we had to win out to keep our season alive. We've knocked down seven of the eight, we just have one more to go."

— LB Clark Haggans

Brett Keisel recorded sacks of Jake Plummer on back-to-back plays in the fourth quarter, and the second caused a fumble that was recovered by Travis Kirschke and set up the Steelers' final touchdown.

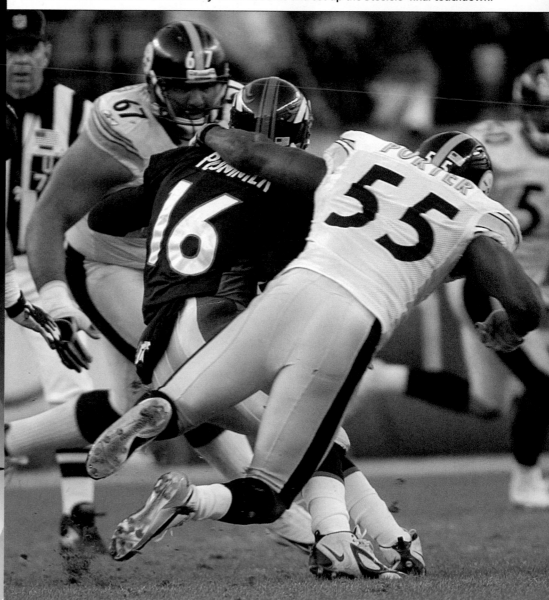

Joey Porter had caused a Plummer fumble with a sack of his own in the first quarter, and that turnover also led to a touchdown.

Defensive coordinator Dick LeBeau makes some halftime adjustments as his players look on.

Ben Roethlisberger punctuated the victory by diving into the end zone for a 4-yard touchdown run that closed out the scoring in the final three minutes.

The games that end with trophy presentations are the ones that require great quarterback play, and Ben Roethlisberger delivered. The Broncos committed to stopping the run early, and so the Steelers again put the ball in their quarterback's hands. He completed 6 of 7 for 77 yards in the first quarter; 13 of 17 in the first half. On a third-and-8 from the 12-yard line, the Broncos blitzed, but Roethlisberger moved Champ Bailey with a pump fake and then dropped a rainbow into the corner of the end zone for Cedrick Wilson, who secured the ball and got his feet down for the touchdown that gave the Steelers a 10-0 lead. Roethlisberger finished with two touchdown passes, and he ran for the one that iced the game.

In the first halves of the three playoff games, Roethlisberger has completed 34 of 49 (69.4 percent) for 486 yards, with six touchdowns and one interception for a passer rating of 132.3. And one more: on third down, he's completing 70.4 percent, with four touchdowns and no interceptions.

— Game reports

Somebody could change coaches and still win, but doing it the way we do it is us. The way we do things, and the way our organization puts things together and looks at things, stability is an important thing.

We have Bill Cowher and the coaching staff, and they're excellent. We have Kevin Colbert, who has done a marvelous job of picking players. This is the way we do things, and it works for us.

Now we have Art coming onto the scene and making decisions. We have a young organization, but also one that has a lot of maturity and background in the business.

— Dan Rooney

Team chairman Dan Rooney accepts the Lamar Hunt Trophy from former Miami quarterback Bob Griese, much to the delight of Coach Bill Cowher; team president Art Rooney II shares a moment with Jerome Bettis in the victorious locker room.

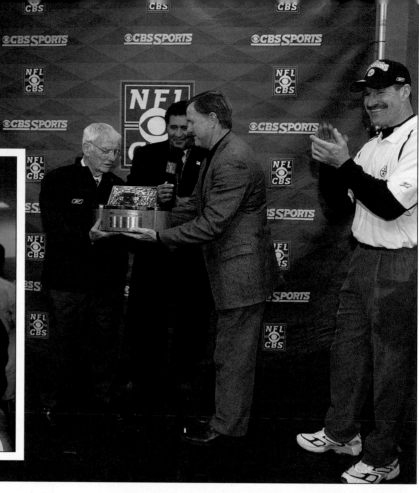

Ben Roethlisberger and Bettis proudly showed off the fruits of their labor after the Steelers became AFC champions.

Safety Troy Polamalu and linebacker Joey Porter took their turns smiling for the camera with the AFC Championship trophy in hand.

Offensive tackle Max Starks acknowledges the large group of Steelers fans who had made their presence felt at Invesco Field.

Super Bowl XL

Big plays the difference

Pittsburgh is a different place during football season. It's even more different come playoff time when the Steelers are involved. But the Steelers in the Super Bowl is a whole other matter, because that's when the mania infects every facet of daily life. Church, school, definitely at work, all over the wardrobe, and constantly in social settings.

The players who got the team to Super Bowl XL had surpassed matinee-idol status to the degree that an appearance even by a couple of them couldn't be announced too far in advance because of crowd control issues. The local newspapers had hours worth of staff meetings to "coordinate coverage," the radio stations amped it up with a variety of fight songs, and the television news departments lost their minds totally.

Apparently, the Super Bowl also is a different event when the Steelers are involved. Detroit Police Commissioner Ella Bully-Cummings held meetings the day after the Steelers had won the AFC championship because she knew it was an easy drive between her city and Pittsburgh, and so she considered it a real possibility there could be as many as 100,000 extra Steelers fans coming in for the game even though they had no tickets nor any real interest in acquiring any. Hotels were sold out as far away as Toledo, Ohio, and merchandisers were salivating, because a Steelers win could mean a 300 percent increase in sales, maybe more.

Meanwhile, the Steelers players and coaches just kept grinding, as they had been for seven straight weeks. About nine hours after the Steelers' charter touched down after the trip home from Denver, the players and coaches had gathered for a meeting at the UPMC Sports Performance Complex. Dan Rooney stood at the front of the room and set the tone. One of the points he emphasized: Forget all

that "One for the Thumb" garbage. This Super Bowl has nothing to do with the four trophies in that glass case down the hall. That team was that team, he told them, and this team has its own identity. This is your Super Bowl.

This was their Super Bowl, yes, and so it was going to be handled like any other game. Winning was the only focus, and that emphasis came through in the first couple of decisions they made. With the AFC as

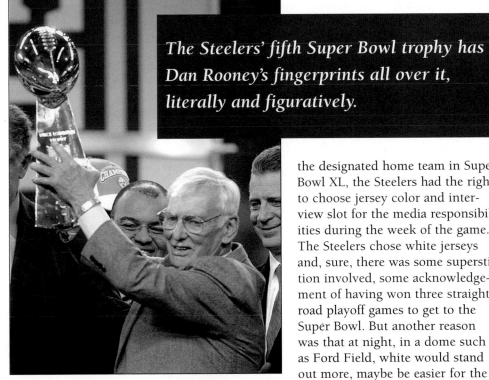

The Steelers' fifth Super Bowl trophy has Dan Rooney's fingerprints all over it, literally and figuratively.

the designated home team in Super Bowl XL, the Steelers had the right to choose jersey color and interview slot for the media responsibilities during the week of the game. The Steelers chose white jerseys and, sure, there was some superstition involved, some acknowledgement of having won three straight road playoff games to get to the Super Bowl. But another reason was that at night, in a dome such as Ford Field, white would stand out more, maybe be easier for the quarterback to pick out. Then, choosing the early interview slots allowed the players and coaches to have completely uninterrupted days of work in Detroit.

The Steelers were in this Super Bowl, and as usual they did things their way. The NFL suggested the teams arrive in Detroit on the Sunday before the game; the Steelers arrived Monday afternoon and traveled with no more amenities than they had on their flight to Houston back in September. On Media Day, the NFL had provided police escorts for the buses that transported the teams from their hotels to Ford Field for the event. But Media Day to the NFL is nothing but Tuesday morning rush hour for a lot of regular working stiffs, and the big-shot treatment made Dan Rooney a little grumpy. "Why are we in such a big hurry? To come here for this. Those were people just trying to get to work so they can pay their bills."

Dan Rooney had his fingerprints all over the things that were done to turn the Steelers into a dynasty during the 1970s, but those Super Bowls were his father's. Art Rooney Sr. had founded the franchise in 1933 and was one of the men who built the league, he was an active Hall of Fame member, and so when it came time to take a bow, nobody deserved it more. Dan Rooney's son, Art II, had been named the team's president in 2004, and his fingerprints were all over the things that were done to get the Steelers into Super Bowl XL, but it just wasn't his time. Dan Rooney had been inducted into the Pro Football Hall of Fame in 2000 because he helped build the free agency/salary cap formula that turned his father's NFL into the professional sports league that was the model for all the others. This bow would be his, and nobody deserved it more.

But there was that other story line, too. The one about the guy who was going home for a shot at a championship in what most people believed was going to be his last game. The Jerome Bettis story, the one being told all over the world, literally, in languages left with the task of trying to translate "bus." In

One of the biggest stories of the Super Bowl involved Jerome Bettis, and it had a happy ending.

the Jan. 25 issue of the *Detroit Free Press,* columnist Mitch Albom wrote, "The Steelers are clearly Detroit's choice, and if you pushed me to give you one good reason, I'd hem and I'd haw, then I'd give you 100. The first 50 are Jerome Bettis. He is from Detroit. He went to school in Detroit. His parents live in Detroit. He eats. He smiles. He knocks people over.

"He's as close as we get to a Lion in the Super Bowl. Besides, Bettis cemented his favorite son status on the sidelines Sunday, when he screamed, "We're going home!" We are not used to people being that excited about a trip to Detroit. Usually, it's, 'Aw, do we have to?' ... Ben Roethlisberger is our kind of quarterback ... Then there's Bill Cowher. Are you kidding me? He's the football coach this town has been coveting for the last 30 years. We want them tough. We want them angry ... Did we mention ownership? The Steelers have the kind of ownership Detroit fans dream about ...

"The Steelers are our choice. We have adopted them as if they were our own. Come next week, Detroit will feel like a home game for Pittsburgh."

It did. The announced paid attendance for Super Bowl XL was 68,206, and 40,000 of them were Steelers fans. Easy. The twirling Terrible Towels obliterated any patches of Seahawks fans, and the noise level matched what the eye could see. And you could tell a lot of them were long-time Steelers fans, because they booed Ray Lewis of the Baltimore Ravens and Larry Brown of the Dallas Cowboys during the introductions of past MVP winners, and they booed when New England quarterback Tom Brady was recognized as the man to toss the coin.

It didn't look like a road game on the field for the Steelers, either, especially not like the road playoff games they had won to get there. The pressure of the situation, the magnitude of the game and its potential to label the guys in it as winners or losers for the rest of their careers had set in. Players were tight. One of those was Ben Roethlisberger, and with the quarterback it's always the most obvious.

Two of their first four offensive snaps began with false starts, and the Steelers went three-and-out on three straight possessions. Two plays after they recorded their initial first down, the Steelers turned the ball over. After the trophy presentation, Roethlisberger would take a moment in the locker room when he sat alone, apparently reflecting on his first Super Bowl, and his body language said he was disappointed. Based on his development through the regular season and the way he blossomed through the AFC playoffs, he had every right to be disappointed. But even on a day when his overall performance fell below his expectations, Ben Roethlisberger still made a handful of big plays that were very, very important to the Steelers' 21-10 win over the Seattle Seahawks.

The first example was the Steelers' possession following that interception. While the offense had been struggling, the Steelers defense may have given up some yards but the Seahawks had managed just a field goal through five possessions themselves and, in fact, Seattle punted the ball back to Pittsburgh three plays after Roethlisberger's interception.

On a third-and-6, Roethlisberger scrambled and then shoveled the ball to Hines Ward to convert and keep the drive alive; then on a third-and-28, he had the awareness to keep his scramble behind the line of scrimmage and then made an amazing athletic play to get the ball all the way across the field to Ward for 37 yards to the Seattle 3-yard line; and he capped the drive when he threw his body into the end zone on a quarterback sweep for the touchdown and a 7-3 lead at halftime.

It became 14-3 on the second play of the second half, and that 12-second snippet served as testimony to the value

ed in points allowed than yards allowed. The game would end with Seattle scoring on only two of its nine possessions that crossed into Steelers territory, and this one would be stopped by a takeaway.

Coordinators Ken Whisenhunt and Dick LeBeau both had a lot to do with the Steelers reaching the Super Bowl, and so it was only fitting that both of them would come up big in the season's biggest game. In the three playoff games, Joey Porter had three sacks, and on a third-and-18 from the Steelers 27-yard line it had seemed certain he would be rushing the passer. But LeBeau called a defense that dropped Porter into coverage, and when Seattle quarterback Matt Hasselbeck tried to get the ball over Porter, it was overthrown and intercepted by Ike Taylor.

Coordinators Ken Whisenhunt (r.) and Dick LeBeau both had a lot to do with the Steelers reaching the Super Bowl, and so it was only fitting that both of them would come up big in the season's biggest game.

of having instilled the mind-set to run the football on offense. Alan Faneca and Jeff Hartings opened the seam; Max Starks came down and sealed it with a block on the middle linebacker; Willie Parker hit it at top speed; and when the safety was a little too aggressive and took the wrong angle, it was over. A Super Bowl-record 75 yards, and if the Steelers weren't the smoothest operation that day, they were practicing what Cowher always preached — finding ways of doing the things necessary to win.

The Steelers' control of the game, however, would evaporate on their next offensive possession. After Seattle kicker Josh Brown missed his second field goal of the game, this from 50 yards, the Steelers seemingly found their offensive rhythm. Roethlisberger completed 2 of 3 for 31 yards and Bettis carried four times for 22 more to set up a third-and-6 from the Seahawks 7-yard line. Roethlisberger underthrew Cedrick Wilson in the flat in a situation where air under the ball meant a certain touchdown and a game-clinching 21-3 lead, and cornerback Jimmy Herndon returned the interception a record 76 yards to the Steelers 20-yard line. When Jerramy Stevens hung on to a 16-yard pass three plays later, it was 14-10, and the Seahawks were breathing the sweet air of new life.

Again, the Steelers offense settled into a funk. Two more three-and-outs brought the game to the end of the third quarter, and then early in the fourth, the defense did its thing. The Seahawks had been having regular success moving the football, but the Steelers clearly were more interest-

Four plays later, on a first-and-10 from the Seattle 43-yard line, Whisenhunt went with "Fake toss 39, X reverse pass." A perfectly timed call of a play that included a beautiful throw on the dead run by Antwaan Randle El to Ward for the 43-yard touchdown, but it also was a play that opened up only after Roethlisberger made another of his big plays — a block on snooping safety Michael Boulware. It was 21-10, and then the Steelers spent the last 8:56 of the game being the Steelers — their defense had a sack to force a punt on Seattle's ensuing possession, then their offense chewed up 4:24 on the clock, and the defense closed it out by turning the ball over on downs with three seconds left.

Hines Ward was named Super Bowl MVP, and that was fitting because he had become the face of the traits so many of them brought to every game, the way they were tough and physical and competed with every fiber of their being. But it also could have been Faneca or Randle El or Casey Hampton, and those choices would have been OK, too, because what they all truly wanted most was to be part of a championship team.

Then it was time to celebrate. And celebrate they did, into the night, on the flight back to Pittsburgh the day after the game, during a parade the day after that through Downtown Pittsburgh attended by 250,000 people. The Pittsburgh Steelers were Super Bowl champions for the fifth time in franchise history, and they won this one as a No. 6 seed in the AFC, by becoming the first team in NFL history to do it all on the road. The 2005 Steelers had done what Dan Rooney had told them to do in that meeting almost two weeks before — they had made Super Bowl XL their own.

The Steelers continued their tradition of honoring a player or coach by wearing someone's throwback jersey when they donned Jerome Bettis' Notre Dame jersey on the flight to Detroit. Bettis also wore his Notre Dame jersey, along with the jacket and cap of his hometown Detroit Tigers.

While guys like Ben Roethlisberger and Jerome Bettis drew quite a crowd during Media Day, practice squad player Richard Seigler had the chance to enjoy some free time and take in the scene.

The Steelers get ready to pose for their official Super Bowl team photo. Injured linebacker Andre Frazier (94) trades places with fellow linebacker Ronald Stanley (47) to spare him from having to climb to the top row.

The media got a lot of mileage out of the verbal sparring between linebacker Joey Porter and Seattle tight end Jerramy Stevens, even though it was much ado about nothing.

The Steelers practiced at the Silverdome in the week leading up to the Super Bowl, but the defensive backs still found time for a little clowning around.

Game Day

Jerome Bettis continued his practice of showing up for a game away from Heinz Field elegantly dressed, and he was joined on this occasion by Joey Porter (l.) and Duce Staley.

If the Steelers quarterbacks were nervous the day of the game, they did a nice job of not showing it.

In the minutes before it was time to step onto the field, Alan Faneca went over the game plan again, Jerome Bettis used a nebulizer for his asthma and Ike Taylor just chilled.

Bill Cowher addresses his players one last time before the Steelers run out onto the field for the start of Super Bowl XL.

SUPER BOWL XL

SEATTLE 10
PITTSBURGH 21

Date: Feb. 5

Site: Ford Field

Outdoor weather:
30 degrees

Steelers leaders
Rushing:
Willie Parker,
10 carries for 93 yards, 1 TD
Passing:
Ben Roethlisberger,
9-for-21 for 123 yards,
0 TD, 2 INT
Receiving:
Hines Ward,
5 catches for 123 yards, 1 TD
Defense:
NT Casey Hampton,
4 tackles, 1 sack

The pregame festivities featured, among other things, music by the legendary Stevie Wonder as well as recognition of the previous Super Bowl MVPs — including former Steelers running back Franco Harris.

Because of what Jerome Bettis has meant to the Steelers, his teammates decided to let him have his moment in the spotlight by running out of the tunnel by himself.

One of the storylines last week was how the result would impact Bill Cowher's legacy. Well, it's not a stretch to believe this win bought him 15 more years with the Steelers. That's enough time to set up shop on Mount Rushmore.

If Cowher averages 7.33 wins in each of those 15 years, he'll move past Tom Landry into third place on the all-time win list for coaches. The list then would read: 1. Don Shula 328; 2. George Halas 318; 3. Bill Cowher 251. Cowher would be 63 years old at the time.

If Cowher averaged 0.6 playoff wins per 15 years, he'll move past Landry as the all-time post-season winner.

We might be in the middle of one of the greatest coaching reigns in NFL history.

— By Jim Wexell

Hines Ward got the votes and left with the car, but this championship has been about the little things. Antwaan Randle El threw that 43-yard touchdown pass to Ward; he made the catch on third down that gave the Steelers their initial first down of the game, in the second quarter; his 12-yard punt return started the first touchdown drive; he turned a third-down slip screen in the fourth quarter into a clock-munching first down; and he was the one who saved a touchdown when he ran down Kelly Herndon after the second of two Ben Roethlisberger interceptions.

◆◆◆

The Seahawks, who led the NFL with 57 touchdowns during the regular season, had 12 offensive possessions in the game. Nine times in those 12 possessions, they either drove the ball into Steelers territory or took over in Steelers territory. On seven of those nine possessions, they scored no points.

— Game reports

Three plays after Hines Ward came down with a 37-yard pass to convert a third-and-28, Ben Roethlisberger gave the Steelers a 7-3 lead midway through the second quarter when he scored on a 1-yard touchdown dive.

| SEATTLE | 10 |
| PITTSBURGH | 21 |

Key moment: The Steelers led 14-10 when the Seahawks found themselves in field goal range early in the fourth quarter. But Ike Taylor intercepted Matt Hasselbeck on third-and-18 and four plays later Antwaan Randle El threw a 43-yard touchdown pass to Hines Ward to pretty much put the game away.

Steelers Digest Player of the Week:
WR Antwaan Randle El

Quote to remember:
"Our football team earned this. Seattle is a great team. We played great teams all throughout the playoffs. We just hung in there and tried to have character of stone where it is not going to break. We pushed on through, gave great effort and we came out with a victory and we are now Super Bowl Champs 2006."

— LB Clark Haggans

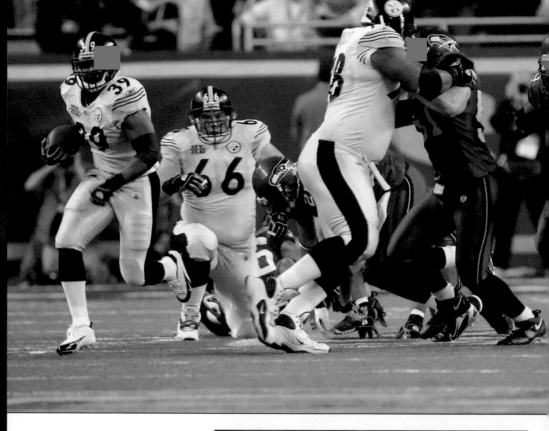

Thanks in part to a great block by All-Pro guard Alan Faneca (66), Willie Parker put himself in the Super Bowl record book with his 75-yard touchdown run, which gave the Steelers a 14-3 lead early in the second half.

I know a lot of people looked at us as if we were favored in the game. It was a little scary going in because when you watched Seattle and what they've done, I don't know if they did get enough credit for what they'd done.

I knew it was going to be a tough game. I think our players knew it was going to be a tough game. (The Seahawks) are a well-coached team. They will be back. I've got so much respect for them.

As for our team, for Hines Ward to get the MVP award, I think it's indicative of our football team. You talk about guys being unselfish, you talk about guys being tough, Hines Ward represents all that.

I said before, in my 14 years in Pittsburgh, we've had good teams, we've had confident teams, but this was the closest team we've ever had.

— **Coach Bill Cowher**

With these guys, Dan Rooney wanted to win for the fans, and Bill Cowher wanted to win for Rooney, and Joey Porter wanted to win for Cowher, and a whole bunch of other guys wanted to win for Dick LeBeau or Kimo von Oelhoffen, and everybody wanted to win for Jerome Bettis.

Once it's personalized, this fifth Lombardi Trophy in franchise history will speak of a team that won without dominant talent coached by a man who directed it masterfully. These Steelers are the champions, not because they necessarily were the best but because they were better at the opportune time, and that's the only way to win in a league where parity has become a fundamental truth.

— **By Bob Labriola**

"I'm officially retired. It's official like the referee's whistle."

— **Jerome Bettis**

The Steelers had great success with trick plays throughout the year, but none was bigger than Antwaan Randle El's 43-yard touchdown pass to Hines Ward midway through the fourth quarter.

The Steelers defense came up with a couple of big plays in the fourth quarter to preserve the lead, including Ike Taylor's interception at the 5-yard line and a Deshea Townsend sack on third-and-8 from the Pittsburgh 47-yard line.

Bill Cowher got a well-deserved Gatorade bath after the Steelers' fifth Super Bowl title was secured.

While the Steelers were busy making their halftime adjustments, the Rolling Stones entertained the crowd at Ford Field and those watching on television with a mini-concert that included the song "Satisfaction." A couple of hours later, the Steelers were feeling a whole lot of satisfaction.

Post-Game

There was a lot of hugging after the clock ran out, and offensive coordinator Ken Whisenhunt made sure to find quarterback Ben Roethlisberger.

Casey Hampton Jr. gets a victory ride on dad's shoulders.

"It's great. I wish everybody could experience this, truly. It's one thing to be the best team in the world for this season, and we are so blessed. I believe we deserved it because we were a team. There were no individuals. We were a team and we played that way."

— TROY POLAMALU

Director of Football Operations Kevin Colbert celebrates with daughters Jenny (l.) and Kacie.

"I'm just happy for him (Dan Rooney). It was for him. He's a special guy and I'm happy for him, the city of Pittsburgh, and he's what's right about the National Football League. I'm very fortunate and blessed to work for a guy like that. He's a very inspired individual. He looks at you and he makes you want to work as hard as you can to succeed."

— BILL COWHER

Super Bowl MVP Hines Ward and Jerome Bettis both had the privilege of going up to the podium at Ford Field to hold up the Lombardi Trophy.

"It feels amazing. To be able to win this, here with Jerome (Bettis) in his hometown and with the offensive linemen and all of the other guys that put in a lot of work — it's just absolutely amazing. I finally get to shave, so I can't wait."

— BEN ROETHLISBERGER

"This championship is great for so many people. It's great for the Rooneys, it's great for Coach Cowher. That was his only knock, that they said he couldn't win the 'big one,' so you can't say nothing bad about the guy anymore. Jerome Bettis played in his final game and that was the best way for him to go out. Anybody that you guys doubted, the doubt is officially erased. And if you don't erase it, there's nothing we can do about it. We won the ultimate game today, the Super Bowl."

— JOEY PORTER

The Steelers celebrated their Super Bowl victory on Sunday night with a party at the team hotel that featured a concert by The Commodores. Bill Cowher, along with wife Kaye and daughter Meagan, also got the chance to mingle with Hank Williams Jr. (bottom left) and Kid Rock (bottom right).

Parade

It was all Steelers in Pittsburgh in the early part of February, and approximately 250,000 people made their way to the downtown area the day after Super Bowl XL as the city celebrated the team's fifth world championship title.

There were smiles all around that day as Steelers players and coaches paraded through the streets and proudly showed off the Vince Lombardi Trophy.

FreezeFrame

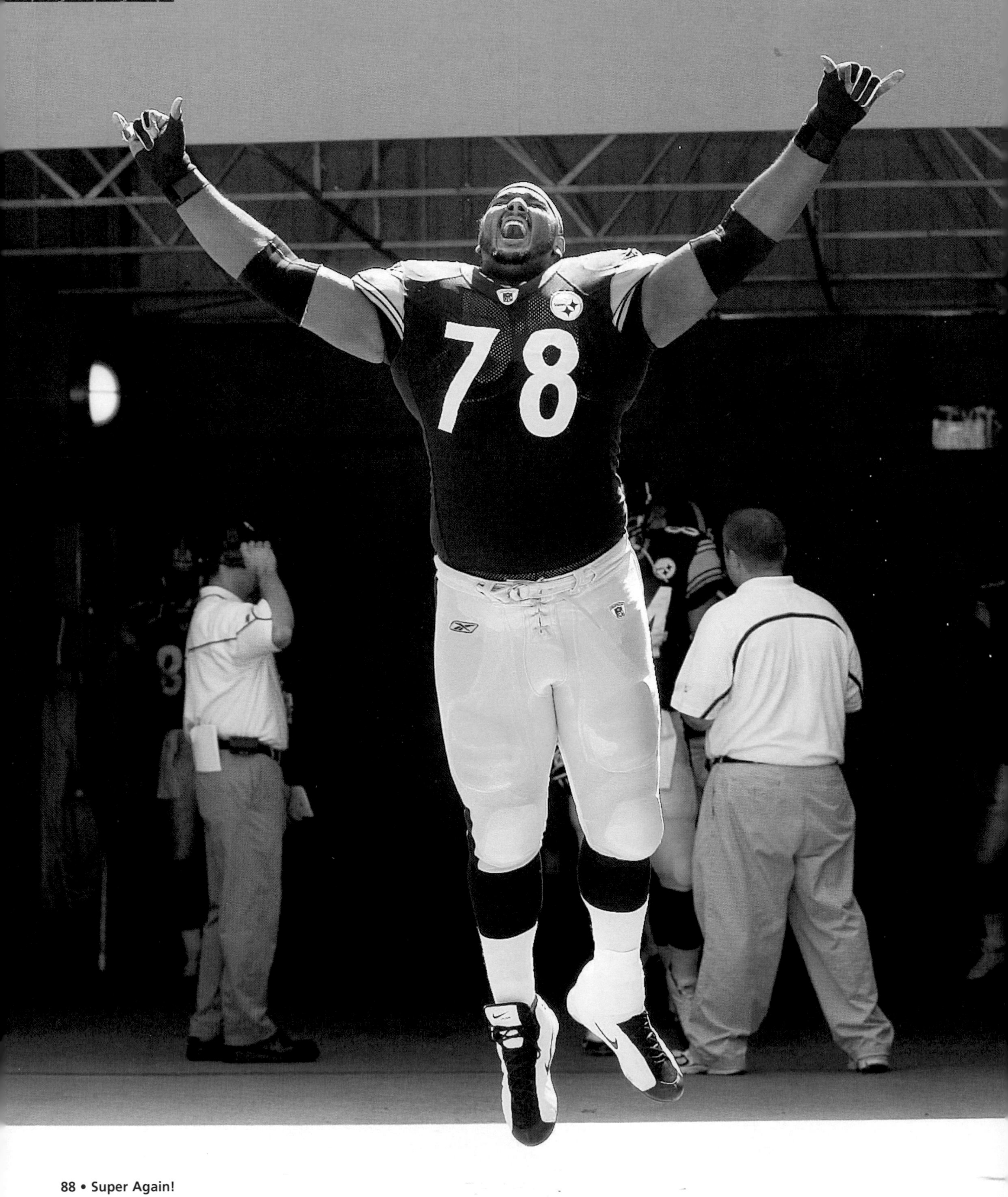

erome Bettis

A winner in every sense

The best player in franchise history. The best team. The biggest win. The most disappointing loss. The most passionate rivalry. Since the Pittsburgh Steelers were founded in 1933, there has been a lot of football played by a lot of guys, and that means it can be difficult to reach definitive conclusions about much of anything. Except in one area.

The best trade in Steelers history happened on April 20, 1996, the day of that year's NFL draft. In the trade, the Steelers sent their No. 2 pick in that draft and a No. 4 pick in 1997 to St. Louis for the Rams' No. 3 pick in the 1996 draft and a 24-year-old alleged has-been running back named Jerome Bettis. You see, the Rams didn't need Bettis anymore because they had used the sixth overall pick in the 1996 draft on this can't-miss I-back from Nebraska named Lawrence Phillips, while the Steelers were looking for a big back to replace Bam Morris. Nobody from the Steelers was indicted for robbery that day, and the statute of limitations since has expired.

"It's a bit of a relief for me, because I didn't want to be relegated to a backup role or possibly have to play fullback when I know I'm capable of running the football," Bettis said on the day of the trade. "That was the frustrating part for me. I wanted to try to get the deal done so that I could look forward to running the football again. I'm just elated that the deal could go through."

Bettis' words proved prophetic, because he went and proved he had 10 more NFL seasons in his body, and during that time he played in 145 more games and carried 2,683 times for 10,571 yards and scored 78 touchdowns. Those numbers don't include the 13 playoff games in which he carried 199 more times for 675 more yards and nine more touchdowns.

His 13-year career began as a first-round draft choice from Notre Dame and ended after the 2005 season, and his 13,662 yards leave him fifth on the NFL's list of all-time rushers, but with Jerome Bettis it's always been about more than statistics.

Jerome Bettis retired from the NFL while standing on the podium at Ford Field with the Lombardi Trophy in his hands, and that's not the only reason Bettis will be remembered as a man who retired as a champion. He was a leader in the locker room, an example, a mentor, a friend, a teammate through each of his 10 seasons with the Steelers. Ask Verron Haynes sometime about Jerome Bettis' influence on his career. Ask Willie Parker about the time during his rookie year when Bettis took him to an upscale restaurant so the next time in that situation wouldn't be Parker's first time. Ask all of them about how Bettis has helped them become a better player.

"He had a lot of influence, he just helped me out in a lot of ways," said Parker, who became the only back besides Bettis to post a 1,000-yard season during Bettis' decade with the Steelers. "He told me that in running to the outside, you have a lot of speed, and that a lot of people will think that you will go to the outside because I have speed. But he told me what I can really kill them at is when I run inside. He said inside runs are where long runs come from. It is hard to break a long run on the outside in the NFL, because everybody is fast in the NFL."

Bettis is the guy who took a pay cut in back-to-back seasons because he couldn't envision himself playing for a team other than the Steelers; he's the guy who welcomed Duce Staley to the team even though it was obvious the Steelers signed him to be a starter; he's the guy who so moved Staley that Staley went to Coach Bill Cowher midway through the 2005 season and offered up his own playing time. And through it all, Bettis gave back to the community, much of it through his The Bus Stops Here Foundation that was founded in 1996 to help underprivileged children.

"His character is so great. To me, he is the NFL," said defensive end Brett Keisel, a seventh-round draft choice from BYU in 2002. "He is everything that I think the NFL wants to be. He is professional, he's very well-spoken, he's unselfish and he is everything guys try to be in this league. He's a great example for all of us, for all the things he does for the team and all of the things he does for Pittsburgh. He is just invaluable to this team."

And besides providing college tuition assistance through The Jerome Bettis Scholarship, and teaching fundamental life skills at The Jerome Bettis Pro Football Camp, and getting inner-city kids hands-on computer experience through the Cyber Bus Computer Literacy Program, the guy could play football.

"He's a fit here," Bill Cowher said in October 1996. "We're a hard-nosed football team. That's how we approach the game — with a no-nonsense attitude — and that's the way Jerome is. When Jerome came here, he really didn't stand out because he fit in. He fit in with the type of people we have around here. Those are people who recognize the difference between when it's time to play and when it's time to work. When you look around our locker room, those are the kinds of people we have. He was a natural fit. When you can get a guy to come in from another team and he fits, it really is an uplift for your team. The talents that Jerome has, and the way he has spoken without saying a word on Sundays, that's the best type of leadership you can get."

But leaders only have credibility if they first prove to their teammates that they're players. Bettis was voted Steelers MVP after each of his first two seasons following the trade to Pittsburgh; he posted six successive 1,000-yard seasons; and he led the team in rushing after eight of his 10 seasons here. And understand that while Jerome Bettis was carrying the football for the Pittsburgh Steelers, he was doing more than just gaining yards. He was setting the tone for the physical style Bill Cowher demanded.

"The most exciting thing," said center Jeff Hartings, "is to see him run over someone in the secondary. By

the fourth quarter, you can tell. They aren't so anxious to hit him anymore."

And so it was through his last game as a professional. In Super Bowl XL on Feb. 5, 2006, in his hometown of Detroit, Bettis carried 14 times for 43 yards, and seven of those carries came late in the fourth quarter after the Steelers had taken a 21-10 lead and all that stood between them and the Lombardi Trophy was the time on the scoreboard clock.

"Jerome touched everybody," said Hines Ward, "every player on our team, some form, some way. He's touched coaches, players, trainers, everybody."

Bettis became the team's inspiration for the 2005 season that ended with a Super Bowl championship, and when Bill Cowher said that these Steelers were the closest team he's had during his tenure as the coach, well, he knew Jerome Bettis was one of the main reasons why.

"At Jerome's house that night there were 30-40 guys sitting around just looking around at each other and we were having this great home-cooked meal," said Ben Roethlisberger about the dinner Bettis hosted for the team at his parents' house during Super Bowl week. "It made it feel like you were with your high school football team when you had your Friday night meals together. It was just neat because everyone was just laughing, joking, having fun and it was really something special. Everyone just kind of sat there as the night went on and just said, 'Wow, this is a special team.' It was a special opportunity, and it was great to be able to do that, and I think that we are a very special and close team."

Jerome Bettis was a driving force behind that, which is why he deserves to be remembered as one of the special players in franchise history. Even players who don't say much always seemed to have something to say about him.

"I have been here six years and no one has been more of a leader on this team than Jerome Bettis," said tackle Marvel Smith. "It's a cliché, but he is the perfect pro. There are a lot of people who look up to him and want to be in his situation and copy what he does on and off the field."

It will have to be a copy, because the original is one of a kind.

ettis: Through the Years

Jerome Bettis chats with running backs coach Dick Hoak during his first minicamp with the Steelers in 1996.

Bettis finished with 10,571 yards rushing and 1,489 receiving in his 10 seasons with the Steelers.

Bettis led the Steelers in rushing in all but two of his 10 seasons in Pittsburgh.

There were several reasons why Bettis' teammates, such as former Steelers quarterback Kordell Stewart, always had great respect for him. Bettis had great passion for the game; he could excel in all types of conditions, as evidenced by his six Pro Bowl appearances; and it also didn't hurt that he took teammates home to his parents' house in Detroit for Thanksgiving dinner in 1998.

ettis: In the Community

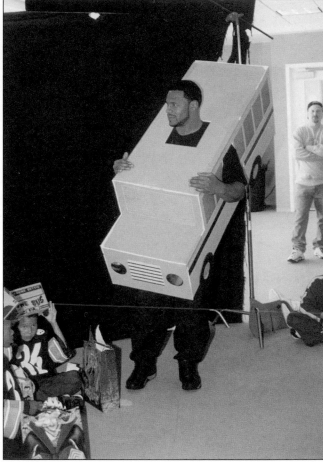

Bettis became so popular with Steelers fans as much because of what he did off the field, and his endeavors included hosting a television show and doing charitable work through his The Bus Stops Here Foundation. Bettis was recognized for his work in 2001 when he was named the NFL Man of the Year.

Bettis: Final Game at Heinz Field

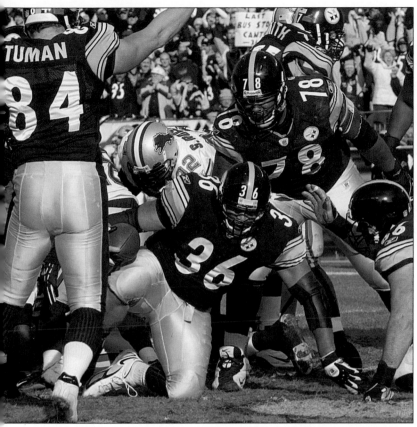

Bettis made sure his last home game would be victorious as he contributed three rushing touchdowns in the Steelers' 35-21 victory over the Detroit Lions.

The end of the game was an emotional time for Bettis, who likely knew at that time he never would play another game at Heinz Field.

Bettis had reason to be pumped after the season-ending victory gave the Steelers a spot in the playoffs.

orld's Greatest Fans

"They are real loyal to the team no matter if you are up or down. Last year when we lost to the Patriots, I think some of them felt worse than we did. It wasn't like, you guys are terrible. They were encouraging and saying we will be all right next year."

— JAMES HARRISON

"I don't know what it is. Everyone just bleeds black and gold. When we lose, the whole city feels down. When we win, you can see the excitement around the city.

Growing up in Atlanta with the Falcons, nobody let it affect them. But when we go out and play well, everyone talks about it during their lunch break and so forth.

They're very passionate about it. Players who played here and move on to other areas, that's one thing they always say — that the city of Pittsburgh has the greatest fans.

They are into the game and they know football. It's a big family. They show us support all the time."

— HINES WARD

"It's their unwavering allegiance to the team and the organization. You won't go anywhere else where you will find fans who travel all across this country, and fans who are not just nationwide, but worldwide. There is a Steelers fan everywhere in this world, no matter where it is you go."

— MAX STARKS

"I have never experienced fans quite like Steelers fans before. They are pretty much going to tell you what's on their mind. They don't hold anything back. Other fans might hold things back, but Steelers fans don't."

— CEDRICK WILSON

"We had a lot of Pittsburgh fans out there (Super Bowl XL) and we loved their support. They were getting pretty loud when we were out there on defense. You've got to give them credit for that. The fans came out in bundles and it really felt like a home game today. All I could see was Steelers fans."

— JAMES FARRIOR

Pro Bowl

The Steelers were well represented at the annual all-star game in Honolulu thanks to Jeff Hartings (64), Casey Hampton (98), Troy Polamalu (43), Alan Faneca (66) and Joey Porter (55).

CHARLIE BATCH
Quarterback

JEROME BETTIS
Running back

BARRETT BROOKS
Offensive tackle

TYRONE CARTER
Safety

RICARDO COLCLOUGH
Cornerback

TRAI ESSEX
Offensive tackle

ALAN FANECA
Offensive guard

JAMES FARRIOR
Inside linebacker

LARRY FOOTE
Inside linebacker

ANDRE FRAZIER
Outside linebacker

CHRIS GARDOCKI
Punter

CLARK HAGGANS
Outside linebacker

CASEY HAMPTON
Nose tackle

ARNOLD HARRISON
Outside linebacker

JAMES HARRISON
Outside linebacker

JEFF HARTINGS
Center

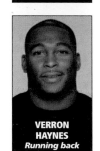
VERRON HAYNES
Running back

CHRIS HOKE
Nose tackle

CHRIS HOPE
Safety

CHIDI IWUOMA
Cornerback

BRETT KEISEL
Defensive end

CHRIS KEMOEATU
Offensive guard

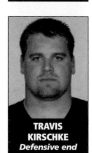
TRAVIS KIRSCHKE
Defensive end

DAN KREIDER
Fullback

CLINT KRIEWALDT
Inside linebacker

MIKE LOGAN
Safety

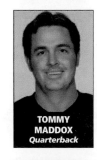
TOMMY MADDOX
Quarterback

LEE MAYS
Wide receiver

BRYANT McFADDEN
Cornerback

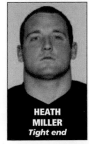
HEATH MILLER
Tight end

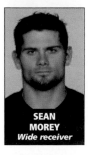
SEAN MOREY
Wide receiver

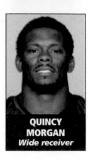
QUINCY MORGAN
Wide receiver

SHAUN NUA
Defensive end

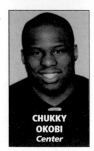
CHUKKY OKOBI
Center

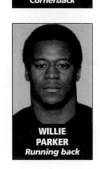
WILLIE PARKER
Running back

TROY POLAMALU
Safety

2005 Pittsburgh Steelers

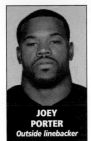

JOEY PORTER
Outside linebacker

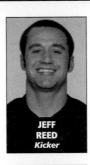

ANTWAAN RANDLE EL
Wide receiver

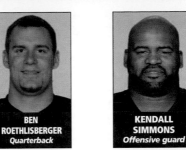

JEFF REED
Kicker

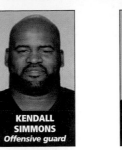

BEN ROETHLISBERGER
Quarterback

KENDALL SIMMONS
Offensive guard

AARON SMITH
Defensive end

MARVEL SMITH
Offensive tackle

DUCE STALEY
Running back

MAX STARKS
Offensive tackle

RUSSELL STUVAINTS
Safety

IKE TAYLOR
Cornerback

DESHEA TOWNSEND
Cornerback

JERAME TUMAN
Tight end

KIMO von OELHOFFEN
Defensive end

RIAN WALLACE
Inside linebacker

HINES WARD
Wide receiver

GREG WARREN
Long-snapper

NATE WASHINGTON
Wide receiver

WILLIE WILLIAMS
Cornerback

CEDRICK WILSON
Wide receiver

Steelers

COACHING STAFF

BILL COWHER
Head coach

DICK LeBEAU
Def. coordinator

KEN WHISENHUNT
Off. coordinator

BRUCE ARIANS
WR coach

KEITH BUTLER
LB coach

JAMES DANIEL
TE coach

CHET FUHRMAN
Cond. coach

RUSS GRIMM
OL coach

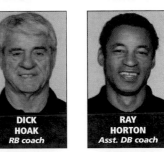

DICK HOAK
RB coach

RAY HORTON
Asst. DB coach

JOHN MITCHELL
DL coach

MARCEL PASTOOR
Cond. assistant

DARREN PERRY
DB coach

MATT RAICH
Off. assistant

LOU SPANOS
Def. assistant

KEVIN SPENCER
Sp. teams coach

MARK WHIPPLE
QB coach

Photo Credits

2005 Season and Super Bowl XL

Mike Fabus, Team Photographer

Karl Roser

Mike Drazdzinski

Dave Arrigo

Jack Wolf (Super Bowl XL)

Ken Keidel (Super Bowl XL)

Photo Assistants

John Fabus

Jonathan Fabus

Michael Fabus

Cover Photo Illustration/Mike Fabus

JUST ONE OF THE 57 BEST TAILGATING RECIPES EVER

PLUS FOOTBALL TRIVIA AND HEINZ FIELD FACTS

TOUCHDOWNS TO TAILGATING

THE RED BOOK FOR ALL YOU NEED TO KNOW ABOUT FOOTBALL, FOOD AND HEINZ FIELD

BY CHARLES REICHBLUM
WITH RECIPES BY RANIA HARRIS

MAKE IT   ORDER IT

Ingredients:
Chimichurri sauce:
10 garlic cloves—peeled
1 bunch flat-leaf parsley—stemmed
3/4 cup olive oil
1/4 cup Heinz® Balsamic Vinegar
1/4 cup chicken stock made from
    Wyler's® Bouillon
3/4 teaspoon dried oregano
3/4 teaspoon dried basil
3/4 teaspoon red pepper flakes
Salt and freshly ground black pepper to taste

Marinade:
3 tablespoons chimichurri sauce
2 tablespoons olive oil
3 whole chicken breasts— halved,
    boned, flattened

Directions:
To make the sauce: In a food processor fitted with the metal blade, purée the garlic. Add the parsley and process until finely chopped. Add the oil, vinegar, stock, and seasonings. Process to blend. Taste and adjust the seasonings. It should be very flavorful and spicy.

In a small bowl, combine all the marinade ingredients and stir until smooth. Put the chicken breasts in a resealable plastic bag and pour in the marinade. Turn the chicken in the bag to coat it evenly. Close the bag and refrigerate for at least 30 minutes or up to 4 hours.

Heat your grill to a medium-high heat or heat a stove top nonstick grill pan. Remove the chicken from the marinade and grill for about 6–7 minutes on each side or until the chicken is cooked through.

Place on a large platter and serve with sauce on the side.

Serves: 4–6

TIP: Use a salad spinner to wash the parsley. The salad spinner not only cleans the parsley well, it also removes all of the excess water.

GET YOUR COPY TODAY! HERE'S HOW

A portion of the proceeds will benefit the Western Pennsylvania Sports Museum at the Senator John Heinz Pittsburgh Regional History Center

Check or money orders:
Make check payable to Knowledge in a Nutshell, Inc.
Cost of each book is $13.90 ($9.95 + S/H), plus applicable sales tax (check one below):

_____ $13.90 + .70 for residents of Allegheny or Philadelphia County = $14.60 total
_____ $13.90 + .60 for residents of all other county residents = $14.50 total
_____ Total

Name: _____

Address: _____

_____

City: _____ State: _____ Zip: _____

For discounts of 10 or more Touchdowns to Tailgating call 1-800-NUTSHELL (1-800-688-7435)

IF YOU WISH TO PAY BY CREDIT CARD, PLEASE CALL 1-800-NUTSHELL, OR SEND CHECK OR MONEY ORDER, WITH COUPON AND YOUR NAME & ADDRESS TO:

Knowledge in a Nutshell, Inc.
1420 Centre Ave. Suite 2213
Pittsburgh, PA 15219

Heinz

GET YOUR COPY TODAY!

For lots of football fun facts, tailgating tips and 57 of the best tailgating recipes ever, get your copy of Touchdowns to Tailgating, written by Pittsburgh radio personality Dr. Knowledge, Charles Reichblum, with recipes by well-known food aficionado and Pittsburgh caterer/chef, Rania Harris.